Slaying the Giant

Practical Help for
Understanding . . . Preventing . . . Overcoming
DEPRESSION

French O'Shields

Cover Design: Portuguese Edition: Wilson Costa, Brazil, Used by permission.
Cover Design: Converted for English Edition: Patrick Powers, SC, USA

SLAYING THE GIANT

ISBN 0-9641901-0-9

Published by: Hem of His Garment
                 P.O. Box 14883
                 Surfside Beach, S.C. 29587-4883

Printed in the United States of America

Dedication

This book is dedicated
to my wife, Alma, who
by her unwavering faith in God
and eternal optimism,
always keeps a light burning
in our window of hope
no matter how dark our world becomes.

Contents

The First Word

There is a giant stalking our land. He threatens each of us. He ruins lives, shatters families, and reduces the work force. He frightens, saddens, and immobilizes. He destroys by convincing us we are helpless and hopeless when in combat with him.

Who is this giant? **DEPRESSION.**

In biblical times another giant stalked the land. The nation was Israel and the giant was the Philistine Goliath. Israel's soldiers, normally mighty in battle, paled with dismay and fear as Goliath shouted his challenge to engage in mortal combat. They resigned themselves to defeat and fled.

Only David, a young shepherd boy — too young to be a soldier — took up the challenge. David against Goliath. An unlikely match. A shepherd, seemingly unarmed against the mammoth Goliath, whose weapons and armor normal men could not even carry.

Man provided David with conventional armor and weapons. He tried them on. They weren't comfortable. He sensed they held little promise of victory. He took them off.

David chose instead his shepherd's sling and small smooth stones he picked from a brook. These stones God created and provided.

As they faced off in battle, the arrogant giant disdained the young shepherd boy. Israel's soldiers — supposedly experts in warfare — thought David insane to think he stood a chance against the giant.

But look! Look! The giant is dead! He is slain by the first stone hurled from David's sling. To all but David, it seemed a most unlikely weapon. One the experts thought would never work.

1

Amazing? Yes indeed. But the real weapon was not the stone. It was David's unwavering trust and confidence in God to give him the victory. In response to Goliath's shouts of scorn, David had confidently replied, "You are coming against me with sword, spear, and javelin, but I come against you in the name of the God of Israel....This very day the Lord will put you in my power; I will defeat you and cut off your head" (I Samuel 17:45-46, TEV). Yes, a spiritual weapon was the real weapon that slew the giant and brought the victory.

In my battle with the giant depression, I discovered the weapons that work best are spiritual weapons. Some of the "experts" may not think so. I know so. I have been there. I know the terror and horror of the battle, and, thank God, I know the joy of victory.

To know more about David's battle with Goliath, read I Samuel 17.

To know more about the giant depression and how to win the battle with depression, read this book.

I am convinced spiritual weapons (spiritual therapy) offer the only complete and lasting victory over psychological depression. I pray God will use this book to convince you also. May *Slaying the Giant* be not only a book you read, but an experience you have.

It is early Easter Sunday morning. I am sitting alone on the deck of the lakeside home of our dear friends Tom and Gail. As I watch the first colorful reflections of sunrise splash on the dark waters of the lake, I am reminded of the resurrections in the life of a Christian. A quiet joy fills me. For sure, to be raised forth into a new life from the grave pit of depression is truly one of the glorious ones.

All praise, glory, and thanks be to God. Through Him YOU CAN OVERCOME DEPRESSION!

French O'Shields
Easter 1994

Introduction

Today you begin an imaginary journey to a strange and foreign world – the world of the depressed.

In reality this strange world is not a place anyone desires or plans to visit, but many of us do. Approximately one out of ten will visit there sometime: male and female, children through old age of every social, economic and educational level. They discover the world of the depressed is not a pleasant place to visit. Life there is horrible, properly described as "a living hell." It is a place to avoid because a real journey there may cost you your life!

Through our imaginary journey, I will tell you how:

...A person gets to the world of the depressed.

...What life is like there.

...How to get back home from this strange world.

WHY TAKE THE IMAGINARY JOURNEY?

Since the world of the depressed is such a dreadful place, why would you ever want to take an imaginary trip there? Taking the imaginary trip is beneficial. It may save a life, yours or someone you love. It will help you:

...Prevent ever visiting this world in reality.

...Return from this foreign land if you are already there.

...To better understand what life is really like for your family member or friend and how to help him return.

YOUR TOUR GUIDE

Before starting any trip you should know your tour guide is qualified to get you there; enable you to experience the place you are visiting; and most assuredly, will be able to get you safely home again.

My name is French O'Shields and I will be your tour guide for this imaginary trip. What are my qualifications? You have a responsibility to know.

In addition to my theological degrees and 28 years experience as senior pastor of three Presbyterian, U.S.A. churches, I have a major in psychology and some training and experience in psychiatry. (For details see About the Author.)

All of this is helpful as your tour guide. But, my most important qualification is I have personally actually been to the world of the depressed. While prone to depression most of my adult life and occasionally experiencing mild depression, in 1985 I suffered clinical depression. I existed, not lived, there for nearly six months. The secular therapy I received was helpful, but it did not get me over my depression. God revealed to me principles, truths, and spiritual exercises that enabled me to overcome my depression and I have been free of it since.

With my training and experience I thought I knew something about depression. Yet, when I became clinically depressed, I discovered I didn't understand what it was like at all. This convinced me that no person can ever know what depression is really like unless he has been there himself. Though I will be sharing with you out of my training and experience, the major portion of what I share will be out of my own personal journey, and what God revealed to me that enabled my return from the world of the depressed.

THIS BOOK

I believe the more a person knows and understands about depression, the more likely he is to avoid or overcome it. So I will seek to tell you much about depression. However, this book is not a scientific treatise or a compilation of quotes from others. Rather, it is to share with you in a simple manner what I have, by God's help, learned about depression with the prayer and expectation that it will bring healing to you, and through you to others.

Out of my gratitude to God for enabling me to overcome my depression, and my compassion for those who struggle with it, I now devote the major portion of my ministry to sharing this through a seminar on UNDERSTANDING, PREVENTING, AND OVERCOMING DEPRESSION. In response to the request and encouragement of many to share this in written form, this book is humbly presented.

PLEASE NOTE:

Some reading this book will be currently in a state of depression. While writing I have been particularly sensitive to these readers. This convinced me to make three choices.

First, thoughts are sometimes repeated in the book. When depressed, one's ability to comprehend is diminished. I can empathize with this and have tried to be alert to it.

Second, I chose not to submit this manuscript to a professional editor for possible rewriting. In some ways it would have improved it. But expressing the depressive's thoughts and feelings in the language in which I experienced them will improve our ability to identify with each other. I consider this more important than eloquence and grammatical perfection.

Third, I wanted the book to read as easily as possible. So when I have needed to write of the depressive in the singular, I have sometimes used the third person pronoun he, him, or his.

This is not intended to denote sex, but a human being, both male and female. It prevents encumbering the text with "he/she" and makes it easier to read.

Please read APPENDIX ONE: ARMORY OF BIBLE VERSES before you begin reading the chapters. This will provide you with a foundation. As you read this book, if you discover any principle or exercise I suggest that is not in accord with Scripture, please dismiss it immediately. If it is confirmed by Scripture, I beg you to accept it as truth, regardless of any preconceived idea you may have had.

— 1

Normal and Abnormal Depression

The man beside me on the airplane introduced himself. Our conversation revealed he practices law, and I teach seminars on depression. "Don't you think everyone gets depressed at times?" he asked. I assured him I did and shared the importance of understanding the difference between normal and abnormal depression.

A line graph of your life experience and mine would look like this:

Living > Change >   Loss > Sadness > Adjust > Growth
                            (normal   (giving up
                            depression) process)

THE PROGRESSION TO NORMAL DEPRESSION

From birth till death, *living* produces *change*. Change is inevitable to living. Life could be described as a continuous series of experiencing and responding to change. A quick glance in the mirror while looking at old photographs will convince any doubters of the reality of change.

Change always produces *loss*. A negative change, such as the death of a loved one or the loss of a job, produces loss.

Even if the change is basically a positive one, it will still have some degree of loss. Most children eagerly await becoming a teen. The teen years appear to them as the promised land. Yet, when attained, they discover they have had to give up some good things about being a child. A girl longs for the day when Mr. Prince Charming will come along and she becomes Mrs. Charming. She soon discovers, as does every married person, that being married provides some wonderful changes, but it also involves giving up some enjoyable things.

Yes, every change we experience in life, whether good or bad, involves some degree of loss.

Loss always produces *sadness.* When we lose something important and pleasurable to us, we experience sadness. This feeling is *normal depression.*

It is experienced by every person because living always produces change, change always produces loss, and loss always produces sadness. Thus, every person who breathes suffers normal depression occasionally.

When loss and sadness occur producing normal depression, it requires us to *adjust* to the change that has produced it. Through a process of giving up the person or thing we have lost, we adjust to the loss. This process involves our total being: mental, emotional, spiritual, and physical. As we successfully adjust to the loss, the sadness will diminish and our depression end. We are able to get on with our life and our *growth* as a person will continue. Normal depression is not intense or prolonged.

We can define a mentally healthy person as one who is able to adjust to change/loss, get on with his life, and thus continue to grow as a whole person.

ABNORMAL DEPRESSION

Depression becomes abnormal and unhealthy when something interferes with our ability to adjust. The giving up process breaks down. For some reason we are unable to complete it and adapt to the change/loss. To us, it seems life has come to a standstill and growth toward wholeness put on hold. The sadness/depression becomes intense and prolonged. This, with all of its accompanying pain, is *abnormal depression*. It is what will be referred to when the word "depression" appears in the remainder of this book.

Not everyone will experience abnormal depression. Some will because adjusting to change is one of life's most important challenges. Change is not easy for any of us.

Many of us in childhood were shielded from losses by our parents. They loved us and did not want us to hurt, so they tried to prevent or diminish our pain. Their intentions were good, but the results not good. We were deprived of learning how to handle loss.

When a child I always had a dog. After a few years of close companionship, my dog always got killed or died. It was the most traumatic loss of my young life. But, I didn't learn a lot about adjusting to loss. Always within a few days, if not the next day, my daddy would bring me a new puppy. My joy over a new puppy shielded me from having to really deal with the pain and hurt of the loss.

The specifics of your childhood losses may differ from mine, but you probably experienced the same shielding by well intended parents. This partially explains why adjusting to change/ loss is so difficult for us as adults.

Depression: Bad, But Not All Bad

Following a hunting accident, I had surgery on my eye. It had to be done under local anesthetic. During the surgery, my eye hemorrhaged, bleeding out most of the deadening drug. My pain was excruciating. So much so, one of the assisting nurses got sick and had to leave. The surgeon, whom I hardly knew, wept as he talked with Alma, my wife, following the surgery because of the intense pain he had seen me suffer.

About 1 a.m. one Sunday (a very inconvenient time for a minister to get sick), I was awakened by a terrible pain. It would ease then return worse than before. Convinced something had to be done, I picked up the telephone beside my bed and called a physician friend. I described my pain, then offered my diagnosis: "I am either having a baby, or I have a kidney stone."

"French, I don't think it is the former," he quickly replied.

"I doubt it myself," I moaned.

Now, admittedly, I have never experienced the pain of giving birth. But women parishioners who have known pain from both childbirth and kidney stones tell me the kidney stone pain is worse. I only know that if it isn't, I sure am glad I can't birth a baby.

A MORE PAINFUL EXPERIENCE

I am acquainted with physical pain. I believe I know what it is. But the intense pain I experienced when clinically depressed exceeds any physical pain I have known. Depression was without doubt the most painful experience I have ever suffered.

Depression is horrible. Most who have been in the world of the depressed describe it as a "living hell." They are right. It is. I know. I have been there.

THE GOOD NEWS

Depression is not all bad. There is some good. Believe me. It does have a positive side.

Depression is to our life what a smoke detector is to our house. Both are warning devices. The smoke detector warns us when something is wrong in our house and demands our immediate action.

Depression also warns us and requires our immediate action. It warns us that something is wrong in our character. There are critical areas of our life in need of repair and improvement. When our life has come to a standstill because of depression, it alerts us to the need to come to grips with the demand for some major personal changes in our character.

YOUR CHARACTER

Character is not defined here as only moral strength or integrity. Rather, it is defined as your complex of especially mental and emotional qualities that distinguish you as an individual. It involves your attitudes, beliefs, life-style, and skills and abilities to respond positively to circumstances. So depression alerts you to the urgent need to repair and improve your life in one or more of these areas.

YOUR OPPORTUNITY FOR A BETTER LIFE

Consider depression a challenge. It can be your opportunity to experience a better life than you knew before you became depressed.

When you successfully make these needed changes in your character and return from the world of the depressed, you will discover a new life — a better life. You will possess an enlarged capacity to:

...Enjoy life every single day. The sky looks bluer, the grass greener, and the flowers more beautiful.

...Envision all the possibilities life has for you. You can walk where you never dreamed possible, even soar with eagle's wings.

...Perceive your life and all that surrounds you in more positive ways.

Yes, there is good news! Depression is not all bad. Being depressed and overcoming it will make life better for you. And YOU CAN OVERCOME DEPRESSION! Believe it! I know. Thank God, I have been there also.

— 3

Depression and the Christian

A woman I did not know wrote to me: "Dr. O'Shields: I am a Christian and I have been deeply depressed for many months. A Christian friend told me real Christians do not get depressed and there must be something wrong with my relationship to the Lord. She said if I were a real Christian I would not be depressed. Is this true? I hurt so bad. Please help me. Sincerely, Mary."

Mary is not alone. It happened to me when I was depressed. Every depressed Christian will sooner or later, usually sooner, receive similar advice. It is devastating. It makes the depression more painful and difficult to overcome. Now Mary not only has to deal with her depression, but also the guilt and anxiety created by the doubt cast on her salvation.

So, it is extremely important for Mary and all of us to know this is not true. Christians can and do get depressed.

Depression, however, is not in and of itself spiritual failure. It does not imply or indicate that you are not a real Christian. Depression is not a sole indicator of whether you are good or bad, but a determiner of whether you are glad or sad.

THE BIBLE AND DEPRESSION

The Book of Psalms in the Bible is a favorite to many. We identify with it because the Psalms express the innermost feelings of a person. One-third of the Psalms, 48 out of 150, speak of depression. The word "depression" may not appear, but the feelings expressed are the feelings of a depressed person.

One good example is Psalm 102:3-7, TEV. Listen to the prayer of this troubled young man express some of the classic symptoms of depression: "My life is disappearing like smoke; my body is burning like fire. I am beaten down like dry grass; I have lost my desire for food. I groan aloud; I am nothing but skin and bones. I am like a wild bird in the desert, like an owl in abandoned ruins. I lie awake; I am like a lonely bird on a housetop."

Some of the Bible's most notable characters experienced depression: David, Elijah, Jonah, Job, and Jesus. Yes, Jesus. In Gethsemane on the eve of His arrest and soon crucifixion, Jesus said to His disciples, "My soul is exceeding sorrowful, even unto death" (Matthew 26:38, KJV). Anyone who has ever been depressed knows there is no better definition of depression than this.

Some of the church's most outstanding leaders have written in their journals of their struggle with depression: Martin Luther, Reformation leader; John Wesley, founder of the Methodist Church; and Samuel Logan Bengle, great saint of the Salvation Army.

NEED TO NOTE

There are two points to grasp with respect to depression and the Christian:

1. Unconfessed, unrepented of, and thus unforgiven sin in our life can cause depression, but not all depression is caused by sin.
2. Even though Christians can and do get depressed, being a Christian does make available to us the resources needed to live free of psychological depression. However, it is not guaranteed. These resources must be appropriated.

CONCLUSION

When someone tells you real Christians don't get depressed, give them credit for good intentions and be grateful they care about you. Then totally disregard and immediately forget what they have said. It simply is not true. It only indicates they know nothing about depression. It is also possible they know very little about being a Christian.

And never, never, never say to a depressed person anything that will cause him to doubt his relationship to Christ because of his depression. Otherwise, you will intensify his depression and make it more difficult to overcome.

— 4

Depression and Temperament

Approximately 10% of the population will experience clinical depression sometime during their life. This means 90% never will. Why is this?

Some individuals are more prone to depression than others. This is primarily due to temperament. We do not all have the same temperament. Therefore, we are not equally vulnerable to depression.

What is meant by a person's temperament? It is the combined mental, emotional, and physical make-up of an individual. It is the complex of mental and emotional qualities that distinguish an individual. It pertains to the manner of thinking, behaving, and reacting characteristic of a specific individual. It is that part of a person referred to when the words disposition, personality, or individuality are used.

As I describe the temperament that is the most prone to depression, you will be able to identify with some of these traits. If you identify with many of them and thus seem to have this kind of temperament, it does not mean depression is inevitable for you. It does mean you are more likely to experience it.

For example, physically we individuals have different bone structure. Some persons have large bones, others have medium bones, and others small bones. The size of your bone structure determines your vulnerability to fractures. But, even if you have small bones and thus are more vulnerable to fractures, you may live to be ninety plus and never break a bone. It doesn't mean you will inevitably break a bone, only that you are more likely too.

The same is true with temperament and depression. Even if you possess some or all aspects of this type of temperament, it does not mean depression is a certainty on your life agenda. You may live your entire life and never experience depression. It only means you are more prone to depression.

So if you have never been depressed, don't start making plans for your own big depression. It may never happen. Hopefully, reading this book and applying it to your life, will prevent it from ever happening.

THE TEMPERAMENT PRONE TO DEPRESSION

In the majority of depressed persons there appears similar temperament traits. This enables us to identify the temperament most prone to depression. You are more inclined to become depressed if you....

1. Are Extremely Introspective

Your thoughts center and focus mainly on yourself. Most all your thoughts turn inward. Usually you are unaware of this. If someone asks you, "Do you realize how much of what you say centers on yourself?" your likely response will be, "Who me? No, not me." This manifests how much a part of you self-centeredness has become. You are no longer able to even recognize it.

2. Are Very Sensitive

Sensitive is not to be confused with sensitivity (an alertness and awareness to the emotions and feelings of others). Rather, for our purpose here, sensitive means fragile feelings. It is the person who is often described as "wearing his heart on his sleeve." To be very sensitive is to be easily hurt or offended by the words or actions, or absence of them, of another person. A particular comment or action that will not faze the ordinary person will be responded to by a person of this temperament with hurt, poutiness, and probably anger.

3. Possess a Negative Self-Image

To have a negative self-image is to have very low self-esteem. You have great difficulty liking and accepting yourself as you see yourself to be. Since you are convinced the way you see yourself is the way you really are, then you automatically assume others don't like or accept you either. After all, if you don't like yourself, you can't conceive of anyone else liking you. As a result, you spend your efforts trying to be the somebody you can like, rather than liking the somebody God has already made you to be.

4. Have Poor Willpower and Self-Control

The preceding traits are always found in this temperament. This one, however, is often present, but not always. When it is, it may incline you toward depression because poor willpower and self-control result in a lack of discipline. The lack of discipline will produce situations that cause you distress, trauma, and guilt. Such crisis situations, coupled with your particular temperament, may be the stone over which you trip headlong into depression. Thus, it is included in the list.

5. Are a Perfectionist

This trait perhaps more than any other disposes you to depression. It is so important and your understanding of it so essential, the entire next chapter is devoted to it.

— 5

Depression and the Perfectionist

Perfectionism was listed as the fifth trait in the temperament most prone to depression. Because it can play a major role in depression, this chapter is devoted to it.

WHAT IS A PERFECTIONIST?

You may be feeling comfortable about now. You may be saying to yourself with a sigh of relief, "A perfectionist I am not!" You are sure anyone who ever saw your closet, kitchen, office, desk, or workshop would never accuse you of being a perfectionist.

Not so fast, you are not off the hook yet. If you could see my desk, it would not suggest "perfectionist." Mess seems to have a way of following me around. Yet, I am an avowed perfectionist. Believe me.

The perfectionist is not a person who does everything perfectly. Rather, he is the person who equates personal worth and value with doing everything perfectly. Thus, he continually demands perfection of himself even though in his eyes he has never achieved it in anything or any way.

Herein lies the problem. If the perfectionist could do everything perfectly, there would be no problem. The difficulty is created not by his actions, but by his expectations. He demands perfection to achieve worth, but is, as everyone else, unable to attain it.

"Perfectionist" is primarily a layman's term. The psychiatrist usually calls it "obsessive compulsive personality." This is not to be confused with "obsessive compulsive disorder" character-ized by irrational behavior such as excessive handwashing. Our use here is far broader. So "perfectionist" is a better term for us.

DESCRIPTION OF A PERFECTIONIST

Observe closely as I draw you a word picture of a perfectionist:

1. The perfectionist adopts a self-formulated and self-imposed set of standards and responds negatively toward himself when he falls short.

2. The perfectionist, because these standards are always unrealistic (not to him), requires himself to be a superman in order to be a man. This means he must be what in the eyes of others would be a "superman," just to be what in his own eyes would be an "ordinary" man.

3. The perfectionist is overly conscientious and requires himself to be accurate and reliable. These are desirable traits for everyone. But to the perfectionist, they are excessively important and obsessive. Here is a practical tip. Don't argue with a perfectionist. You can't win. He must always have the last word because your last word is never accurate.

4. The perfectionist has unrealistic expectations of others, particularly the significant others in his life, and gets angry at them when they don't measure up. Pity the poor perfectionist. He can't get along with himself because he doesn't measure up; he has difficulty getting along with others because they don't measure up. Are you beginning to see what fun it is to be married to a perfectionist or have one for a parent?...Surely I jest!

5. The perfectionist is very structure-oriented. He does not

bend easily. He views any necessary change in or departure from his plans as being a major interruption. The slightest deviation from "the best way" is totally intolerable.

While a pastor, I arrived at my church office each morning with my day planned. Due to my perfectionism, it was always upsetting to me if Mrs. Smith decided to deliver her baby that morning and I had to rush to the hospital. How inconsiderate. Didn't she know my day was already planned?

If a perfectionist asks you to do something, rest assured he will also tell you how to do it. You might as well do it his way. You won't hear the last of it until you do.

6. The perfectionist is greatly controlled by "ought" and "should." This makes it impossible for him to relax.

The wife and mother has worked at her public job all day. She arrives home, fixes supper, straightens up the house, and sits down in the den to watch her favorite television program. But, she doesn't enjoy it. Because she is a perfectionist, as she watches she is saying to herself, "I ought to be doing a load of clothes. I should not be sitting here watching television." So goes the life of the perfectionist.

7. The perfectionist constantly feels some degree of anxiety and tension. Regardless of whether the setting and situation are tranquil or turbulent, the perfectionist will have a gnawing feeling of uneasiness and insecurity. The times are few, if any, that the perfectionist feels really peaceful. His "ought" complex contributes to this.

8. The perfectionist is very critical of self, others, and things, but finds it difficult to receive criticism. His difficulty handling criticism directed toward him is not because he feels it is unwarranted. He is already convinced he doesn't measure up. Rather, it is disturbing to him to realize others are now aware of his

inadequacy. He interprets their criticism as confirmation of his own negative opinions about himself.

9. The perfectionist is never satisfied or feels he did as well as he should regardless of the level of his achievement. Of all the sermons I have preached or pages I have written, I have never been totally satisfied with a single one. I always feel I should have done it better. Intellectually I know over so many years the law of averages had to be to my advantage. There had to be one good one in there somewhere that represented my best. But, not to me. Why? I am a perfectionist, and they are never satisfied.

10. The perfectionist develops a view that he is very inadequate in his being and skills. This conviction is inevitable. It is bound to emerge. When he sets unrealistic expectations for himself, he is going to fail; when he fails, he is going to become convinced he is an inadequate human being.

HOW DO YOU BECOME A PERFECTIONIST?

Behavioral scientists have long debated whether heredity or environment has the greatest impact on our life. The debate goes on. A consensus answer has not been determined.

Both play a part in a person being a perfectionist. You may inherit from your parents certain genes and physical characteristics that dispose you to perfectionism. For example: a tendency toward abnormal thyroid function.

Most assuredly, environment contributes. The persons who sat in my study manifesting perfectionist traits, usually revealed having a parent they could never please, irrespective of notable accomplishments. Perfectionists often beget perfectionists. They create an environment which coupled with heredity, disposes their children to perfectionism.

Does that mean parents should never push their child to

achieve for fear they will make him a perfectionist? No, not exactly. All good parents should encourage their child to achieve at his highest level, but that level should always be based on the child's inherent abilities. Expectations and goals should never be separated from abilities. The pressure and direction of the push must be determined by the inherent ability of the child. Therefore, a wise parent spends the effort and money to have a child's abilities tested and determined before starting to push. This applies to the intellect and to emotional stability and physical dexterity as well.

Many young boys become perfectionists on the little league athletic field by a pushy perfectionist dad who will not be satisfied until his son knocks a home run every turn at bat. It matters not to Dad that his son may have more aptitude for music or art than baseball. He hasn't bothered to find out.

THE GOOD NEWS

Perfectionism is not all bad. Due in part to the perfectionists of the world, all of us enjoy a better way of life. We have cars instead of buggies, lights instead of lanterns, and word processors to replace pen and quill all because of those who were obsessed with creating a better way. No, perfectionism is not all bad, it just needs to be understood and controlled.

Yes, perfectionism can be controlled and changed. It is not set in concrete. You can make this negative become a positive in your life. It is difficult, and it will not occur overnight, but you can change. I have been working at it for years, and even my family agrees I have made some progress – not total victory, but progress.

Ask those closest to you to make you aware when your perfectionism is showing. Often the perfectionist is so caught up in his striving, he is not aware his words and actions are being controlled by his perfectionism.

I make the most progress by talking to myself. At one time this was considered to be a possible sign of insanity. Now books are written on how therapeutic it is. When I put myself down because I have fallen short of my expectation, I have a conversation with myself. It goes like this....

"French, God did not design or create you all-knowing and all-powerful nor will you ever be. Therefore, you do not know all things, understand all things, nor can you do all things. So, French, it is all right for you to fall short of your expectations."

Sometimes I say to myself, "French, to make a mistake is not to be worthless. Your worth is determined by who you are, not by what you do."

When neither of those comments grabs my attention, I resort to this one. Believe me, it always rings the bell. "French, of all the billions of people who have been born into this world, only one, Jesus Christ, has been perfect. Isn't it foolish to think you are the second one? How absurd can you get, French?" Wow, that's telling me!

If your perfectionism is to be changed, you are the only one to do it. You can and should pray for God's help, for without God's help it is impossible. Yet, no one but you can put it into practice. Talk to yourself, and pay attention to what you say.

— 6

Kinds of Depression

Depression is broad in nature. There are different kinds and various levels in each kind. This makes it almost impossible to define in one brief statement. It is necessary for us to attempt it, however, to establish a base line.

DEFINITION

Depression is an overwhelming and all-pervading feeling of sadness, anxiety, and hopelessness usually accompanied, knowingly or unknowingly, by one or all of the three negative emotions of anger, fear, and guilt.

"Overwhelming" and "all-pervading" are accurate descriptive words. The depressed person feels "overwhelmed," dismayed, swamped, and overpowered by this strange feeling. The feeling is "all-pervading" because it touches every part of his being: body, soul (intellect, emotions, and will), and spirit.

TWO KINDS OF DEPRESSION

It is very important for everyone concerned with depression to understand there are two kinds. They are set apart by the initiating cause of the depression.

1. Organic Depression.
This kind of depression is initially caused by an organic or physical impairment or malfunction.

The following are some organic disorders that can cause depression: hypothyroidism (low thyroid function); hormonal imbalance (often involved in depression following childbirth); chemical imbalance in the brain; hypoglycemia (low blood sugar); and a tumor in certain areas of the brain.

Some medical authorities believe depression can also be a side effect of/or accompany other physical illnesses or experiences such as: chronic infection, surgery, coronary disease, heart attack, stroke, and cancer.

Because of the above, most authorities believe that heredity can play a part. This is at times hard to establish, and may apply only to the extent that heredity may dispose a person to one of these physical conditions.

Some medications prescribed for the above physical conditions can as a side effect, play a part in depression.

Statistically, only 10% of depressed persons initially have organic depression.

2. Psychological Depression.

Psychological depression does not initially involve organic causes. Rather, it is precipitated by mental and/or emotional impairment. It involves improper functioning of one's character as "character" is defined and explained on page 11.

Statistically, 90% of depressed persons will initially have psychological depression. So in the vast majority of cases, depression is a psychological concern.

BOTH KINDS

All authorities do not agree there are two kinds of depression. Some believe *all* depression is caused by chemical imbalance. Others, conversely believe *all* depression is psychological and chemical imbalance plays no part. Both views were expressed to me by separate physicians during my therapy. Others believe there are both kinds. The debate has gone on for years with no consensus in sight.

My opinion is influenced by my training and experience, but is basically formed by my own experience with depression. All of this combines to convince me that....

...Initially there are two kinds of depression: organic and psychological.

...Regardless of whether your depression begins organically or psychologically, if it is not diagnosed and treated and thus becomes prolonged, you will eventually have both psychological and organic (chemical imbalance) depression.

After struggling with depression for years (which I believe was totally psychological), there was a specific time when I became aware that my depression had taken on a new and different dimension. At first I did not understand this. Later, I realized the prolonged psychological depression had caused an imbalance in my brain chemistry. Now, I was both psychologically and organically depressed.

It is extremely important for both the depressed person and the therapist to understand this. Failure to do so will impede or possibly prevent the full recovery of a depressed person.

The application here is since a person who has prolonged depression will likely have both kinds, then *both* must be treated. Antidepressants may be needed to get the brain chemistry back in balance, or thyroid medication to balance the thyroid, or the physical illness treated. But, unless the person's psychological depression is also treated, he will not fully be free of depression. If his psychological depression is treated, but the chemical imbalance untreated, he will not fully overcome his depression. This explains why some depressed persons improve, but do not get completely free of their depression.

I cannot overemphasize how important this realization is. It may well be one of the most vital points in this book.

— 7

Levels of Depression

Both organic and psychological depression have various levels. With each level, the depression gets worse and grows deeper. The key factors here are length of time and degree of incapacity. This confirms the importance of early diagnosis and therapy. It may prevent reaching deeper levels.

FOUR LEVELS

There is no consensus on the levels or names for them. I use the following four levels of abnormal depression to help you better understand it:

1. Mild Depression.
This is more than the normal depressive feeling of sadness everyone experiences occasionally. Here more of the classic symptoms of depression appear, but none to an intense degree. It is not chronic. It comes and it goes, but will return. Usually, mild depression is a reactive type of depression triggered by the occurrence of undesirable circumstances or events.

2. Major Depression.
This level of depression comes, but it does not go. It has become chronic. Some days may be better than others, even some times of the same day may be better. But you are never free of this strange and unpleasant feeling. You begin to experience most all of the classic symptoms of depression and to an ever-increasing

degree of intensity. Yet, you are still able, though with difficulty, to fulfill your routine responsibilities. You are able to get up in the morning and go to work, but your family and closest associates detect all is not well with you. You and they realize you are not your usual self.

3. Clinical Depression.

This level is major depression and more. The severity of the symptoms now cause incapacity. You are now unable to function in your normal everyday responsibilities and activities. You are no longer able to go to work. You want to pull the covers over your head in an effort to escape an existence with which you can no longer cope.

It was when my depression reached this stage that I suspected it was something more than psychological. Strange things were happening in and to me. These things I had never experienced before even though I was well acquainted with mild and major depression. I was not only sad, but very frightened because I didn't understand what was happening to me. Whatever it was, I knew it was bad.

4. Severe Clinical Depression.

At this level your inability to function has become so severe, you may become catatonic which is characterized by immobility, stupor, and silence. You give the impression of having lost touch with what is going on around you. You may, or may not, sparingly respond to a direct question or command, but seldom if ever, initiate conversation.

At this severe level of depression, you feel totally hopeless, and your family feels totally helpless. Obviously, if you are not already under professional care, you certainly need to be now. You probably need hospitalization with or without your consent.

LEVELS AND SUICIDE

Sometimes a depressed person will have suicidal thoughts. This may occur at any level of depression, even in normal depression. To have a suicidal thought is not that unusual or alarming, but to *harbor* the thought is.

Suicidal tendencies become stronger as the feeling of hopelessness increases. The more unbearable life appears, the more attractive death becomes. So, normally these tendencies are more prevalent the more depressed one becomes.

There is a commonly held view that the person who talks about committing suicide will never attempt it. This is a myth. It is not true. The person who talks about it may not only attempt it, but also succeed. Never assume any depressed person, even if his depression appears mild, will not attempt suicide.

A depressed person with suicidal tendencies may tell someone or he may hide his thoughts. Because he has not talked about them, doesn't mean he has not had them.

The possibility of suicide must always be taken seriously. Do not rely on your ability to predict it. It is always wise for a therapist, family member, or friend to ask the depressed person if he ever has such thoughts. Some are afraid to do so for fear it will be suggestive. Care and forethought should be taken as to how and when to ask. Hopefully, it can be done in a manner to minimize the suggestive aspect. Even so, it is a risk that must be taken because the cost of not doing so is too great.

If the depressed person acknowledges such thoughts, endeavor to get him to tell you about them. If he indicates he has been planning how and where he may take his own life, this indicates serious suicidal tendencies and demands your immediate action. Do not play psychiatrist. Get him under professional care. If he already is, inform his therapist of what you have learned. Do for the depressed person what he *needs* you to do, not what he *wants* you to do. This is what love demands.

If you are depressed and have recurrent suicidal thoughts, tell your therapist and loved ones. Do not assume you will always be able to control this. Do not be too ashamed to share your thoughts. This is no time to play hide-and-seek. You are depressed and suicidal thoughts are often a part of it. Avail yourself of the help and precautions needed to insure your safety and well-being.

Only a small percentage of depressed persons commit suicide. But even one is too many. Every possible care should be taken to prevent anyone from doing so. Even then, it will still happen sometimes. This is why depression must always be viewed as a potential killer.

PLEASE NOTE: In the remaining chapters "depression" refers to psychological depression unless otherwise noted.

— 8

Triggers of Depression

Depression always has a cause. The depressed person may not be aware of it. His family may not have the slightest clue as to what it is. His therapist may be unable to dig it out. Nevertheless, it does have a cause.

FOUR TRIGGERING EVENTS

Frequently depression develops when one or more of the following circumstances occur and exist in a person's life:

1. A Major Loss.
When you experience a major loss you are forced to give up something of significant value, something that has been an intimate, vital, and meaningful part of your life.

Such losses may be: the death of a loved one, loss of health, a disability resulting from illness or accident, loss of a job, financial reversals, and marriage breakup. These are only a few examples. The list could go on and on.

From Chapter 1 you remember some sadness (normal depression) accompanies all losses. But, when something interferes with the adjusting process and life seems to come to a standstill, the normal feeling of sadness becomes psychological depression (abnormal).

2. Betrayed, Wronged, or Rejected.
To be betrayed, wronged, or rejected by a person or persons whom you love and trust is a devastating experience.

The more significant your relationship, the more ravaging the experience. Ill treatment by a spouse is far more hurtful than by a friend. When a stranger wrongs us, we can brush it off, but when a close loved one wrongs us, it cuts deeply. The degree of the pain is comparable to the closeness of the relationship.

To be betrayed, wronged, or rejected by a significant other, causes hurt, anger, and resentment, creating a fertile field for depression.

3. Bad Decisions.

Bad decisions may include but are not limited to immoral decisions. Any decision which later experience proves to have been an unwise decision, can trigger psychological depression.

Some examples are: bad decisions relative to job, major purchases, retirement, place of residence, marriage, children, divorce, etc.

4. Major Disappointments.

A major disappointment is experienced when a significant event, thing, or person has not turned out as you desired or hoped.

Disappointments disregard age. They occur from childhood through old age.

Adults can't understand how a teen could get so upset over not being invited to the prom or the breakup of a "love" affair. But to the teen, this is loss, rejection, and disappointment all wrapped in one. Such an experience, regardless of how trivial it may appear to "wiser" grown-ups, can be for a teen the launching pad of depression.

Older people, I have discovered, are very vulnerable to disappointments, especially in the form of unfulfilled goals and ambitions. A failed attempt to attain a life's goal even in middle age is not so devastating. You anticipate more years and other opportunities remain. In the latter years, however, you begin to realize the years are running out and certain opportunities are gone forever. It becomes increasingly apparent some of those goals are never going to be fulfilled. It is distressing to have to place unfulfilled dreams in your drawer marked "Never To Be!" It can trigger depression.

IDENTIFYING THE TRIGGER

Not all depression is related to one of these four circumstances. In counseling psychologically depressed persons, however, I have with consistency eventually uncovered the presence of one or more of these four life situations. It does not always immediately or readily appear. The person may not reveal it because he has not related it to his depression. Or, he may intentionally hide it because of pain, guilt, or shame.

There is good news. The triggering event does not have to be identified for healing to take place. When identified, however, it does facilitate the recovery by enabling both the person and the therapist to focus more quickly and thoroughly on crucial matters.

I have found asking questions is the best way to discover if one of these four events is related to the depression. The questions must be carefully worded and inserted into the conversation in a non-threatening manner. I do not ask if he has experienced any of these events. I begin with the assumption everyone has experienced all four. Rather, I word the question to determine the degree of impact the experience has had on his life. These are the four questions I ask, each relating to the four events mentioned above:

1. What do you consider to be the greatest loss you have ever experienced in your life?
2. Who has hurt you more than anyone else in your life?
3. Of all the decisions you have made in your life, which one would you like to change the most?

4. What or who has been the greatest disappointment to you
    in your life?

What he says in answer is important. But, the *time* he takes to
answer, is of greater significance. If it takes him a great deal of
time and thought to come up with an answer, obviously this event
has not had a major impact on his life. This slowness to answer,
however, can be an effort to hide something from you. By
observing closely you can usually discern, however, whether he
really can't remember anything, thus suggesting little or no
impact, or is trying to hide.

If the depressed person responds quickly and with a definite
answer, it indicates this event has had a serious impact on his life.
Encourage him to tell you all he will about the event. A simple,
"Tell me more about that," may be all you need say. If not, you
may need to ask some carefully worded follow-up questions to
help him share with you.

What you discover through these questions and answers may
enable you to identify the trigger, and help your depressed
person gain helpful insights into his depression.

— 9

Symptoms: What It Is Like to Be Depressed

In this chapter I am going to describe how the depressed person thinks, feels, and acts – what life is like in the world of the depressed.

After hearing me teach my first seminar on depression, my wife questioned the wisdom of my talking about the symptoms of depression. Since all of us have a tendency to identify with described symptoms (whether we actually have them or not), she wondered if it would cause people to be depressed.

The last thing I want to do is depress people! So out of respect for her counsel, I did rethink the value of including this.

I concluded describing the symptoms is a must for two reasons. First, to enable the depressed person to know what is wrong with him. Every depressed person is aware something is wrong with him, things are just not right. But many depressed persons do not know the problem is depression. Overcoming depression is easier for the person who is able to identify his depression.

Second, to assist non-depressed persons to better understand what their depressed family member, friend, or patient is going through. To understand what he is thinking, feeling, and why he is acting as he is, will enable you to better help and support him.

CLASSIC SYMPTOMS

I sat in the den of a close friend who was deeply depressed. It was difficult for her to talk. To let her know I understood, I began to describe all she was thinking, feeling, and acting. "Yes," she said, "that's it exactly."

Her husband, who had been present, was amazed and told me later in the yard I had described his wife perfectly.

I assured him this wasn't due to super intelligence. I simply knew what it was like because I had been there.

The symptoms of depression are classic. The old expression if you've seen one, you've seen them all, applies well to depressed persons. Not every depressed person will have every symptom; nor will each person experience each symptom in the same intensity. Though some variation exists, similarity dominates. Most depressed persons feel, think, and act alike.

IDENTIFYING THE SYMPTOMS

Because the symptoms of depression are classic, they are relatively easy to identify. As I describe what it is like to be depressed, I will share with you many of my own experiences.

As you read, notice how these separate symptoms relate to each other. None exists in isolation. It is their nature to feed on each other, thus creating a vicious cycle.

In my training I studied the symptoms of depression, with casual interest, I might add. I never dreamed I would someday be fighting for my life in my own battle with depression. In sharing these with you, however, I am relying more on my personal experience. I know it is real; I have lived it. Yet, I also know it is typical of all depressives.

This is what life in the world of depression is like:

1. A Very Negative Self-Image With Strong Feelings of Inadequacy.

My concept of myself was so low, I felt I could sit on the edge of a sheet of paper and my feet not touch the floor. I was convinced I had failed in every aspect of my life: as a son, husband, father, friend, pastor, and a complete washout as a human being. I recall saying over and over again to my wife, "I am an utter failure in every part of my life. I can't do anything right!"

2. An Overbearing Feeling of Sadness And Negativity.

Sadness and unhappiness overwhelmed me and dominated my feelings and thoughts. Negativity had completely infiltrated my being, robbing me of any joy and gladness. My entire attitude was one of gloom and doom. I would hear people laugh and display signs of happiness. I envied them. I wanted to be like that, but could find no reason to allow myself to do so.

The visual image that kept coming to my mind was a big black cloud that had descended on me, enveloping me, and from which I could not escape. As I have shared this in seminars, it is amazing how many depressed persons have told me of having the same image. It was a 360 degree black cloud; there was no light anywhere.

I developed an uncanny skill to discern something bad in everything. I could find a dark cloud in every silver lining. My wife and others would say to me, "Isn't that wonderful?" or "Wasn't that great?" My reply was always the same, "Yes, *BUT...*" and proceed to point out something negative and sad.

3. Withdrawal.

As depression deepens, so does the desire to withdraw. Eventually, the depressed person does not want to be around other people at all. Attending a church service (I had already resigned my pastorate due to my voice impairment), became extremely difficult. Visits to or outings with friends became unbearable. Though being with immediate family always provided help and support, even this became stressful because of my desire to withdraw.

Depression horribly transforms even a normally gregarious person into a recluse. It turns extroverts into introverts, and introverts into verts – pretty much nothing personality wise.

4. Loss of Interest in Doing Anything.

What does the depressed person want to do? Nothing. Even those things that used to provide much enjoyment and pleasure cease to have any attraction.

I am an avid sports fan. My idea of a super experience is to attend a big football game. Basketball and golf excite me. Baseball raises my pulse, but not as much. But when clinically depressed, I scarcely even watched sports on television. When I did, it held little enjoyment for me. I was too absorbed by my own inner turmoil.

5. Unable to Cope With the Smallest Problem.

I am not referring to major problems. Rather, things so small that ordinarily I would not even call them problems. In my depressed state even the smallest thing to go wrong was viewed as a major catastrophe. Even a fragment of a straw is all it takes to break the back of the depressed person.

6. Unable to Function.

Unless diagnosed and treated, depression may progress to the point the person becomes unable to function. This is clinical depression.

When I experienced this level of depression, the smallest most routine task appeared as Mt. Everest. Even the simplest everyday responsibilities seemed to be insurmountable obstacles.

A hedge runs the length of the yard of my family home into which Alma and I moved following my mother's death. Many years ago my grandfather planted that hedge so it has sentimental value to me. In my depressed state, however, it became a monster. I had to keep it trimmed with hand clippers. It was the fastest growing hedge I had ever seen. Before I could get the clippers back into the tool house, six-inch growth shoots appeared. At least, it seemed that way to me. I remember telling my psychiatrist, "If I thought I had to trim that hedge for the rest of my life, I just as soon be dead!"

Now I can laugh at that comment. Then it wasn't funny; I was dead serious. After my thinking improved and I began to overcome my depression, I bought some electric clippers and now I actually enjoy trimming the hedge. When depressed, it was a task worse than death, all because of my inability to fulfill the most routine responsibilities. Yes, depression is an immobilizer.

7. Indefinable, But Real Pain.

It is not unusual for depression to mask itself as physical complaints such as abdominal pains, headaches, joint pain, back pain, leg pain, etc. Even though there is no organic cause, the pain is no less real.

Most of the time I could not point to any place and say this is where I hurt. This nebulous, but nonetheless real pain was in my innermost being. The pain was far more severe than any physical pain I had ever suffered. I hurt on the inside so bad at times it seemed unbearable, so excruciating I felt I was going to explode.

8. Feelings of Rejection and Being Unloved.

I was surrounded by the abundant and wonderful love and support of my wife, children, and close friends. For this I will ever be grateful to them and to the Lord. Even though I knew I was immersed in love, I still could not totally escape the feeling of being rejected and unloved. It is extremely difficult, if not impossible, to feel loved by others when you don't love yourself. Depression never accepts reality, it distorts it.

9. Feelings of Guilt.

The depressed person always feels guilty. It can, of course, be real guilt if committed sin has not been confessed, repented of, and forgiven. But, often it is false guilt. If there is nothing for the depressed person to feel guilty about, rest assured he will conjure up many reasons. Actually, he will feel guilty about most everything he does or doesn't do. Feeling guilty is an offspring of depression.

10. Very Introspective.

The depressed person is a very introspective person. His thoughts are focused on himself and saturated with self-pity. This self-centeredness is very obvious to others, but the depressed person himself may be blind to it.

11. Indecisiveness.

It is extremely difficult for the depressed person to make even the simplest decisions.

Alma would suggest we go spend the weekend with one of our children and family. I hoped doing so might help me feel better and overcome my withdrawal, so I agreed to go. Now came the arduous part. Because of my indecisiveness, I would literally go through three hours of torment trying to decide what to take in my small bag just to spend one night.

When she would suggest we go to the cafeteria to eat, I reluctantly agreed. I didn't want her to have to cook since my depression was making life hard enough for her anyway. But, I knew what would happen; it always did. I would actually break out in a cold sweat standing in the cafeteria line because I could not decide which vegetables I wanted. The louder the server yelled at me repeatedly, "What can I serve you?...What can I serve you?" (surely cafeteria line servers are required to complete a course in impatience), the more intense my panic became.

Perhaps you have noticed none of these decisions I had to make really mattered. They were not important. But to me, they appeared as matters of life and death. That is depression. It makes every decision seem to be earthshaking in importance. Again, it distorts reality.

12. Anxious and Fearful.

Depression and anxiety are Siamese twins. They always go together. One will always dominate, and thus the problem is either labeled depression or anxiety. But, in either case, regardless of which one dominates, the other is always present.

The anxiety and fearfulness experienced by the depressed person often becomes morbid. He anticipates some impending catastrophe and thinks a great deal about death. I tried to walk several miles everyday because I knew it could help my depression. But my thoughts were so morbid, I feared I would have a heart attack or stroke while walking and be discovered hours later unconscious or dead in the ditch. Trying to avoid such thoughts didn't help; I had them anyway. Depression becomes master of your thoughts.

Another gnawing fear of a depressed person is that of losing his mind, going insane. This fear caused me to envision myself having to be committed to a mental institution. Like most fears of the depressed, it is unfounded. Depression does not normally lead or progress to insanity. Insanity, as most of us picture it, is related to other mental illnesses, not depression.

13. Sleep Irregularities.

Depression interferes with normal sleep. It can go either way. The depressed person may want to sleep all the time, or he may have great difficulty sleeping. For me, it was the latter. I had great difficulty going to sleep, and then if I did, I would wake up often and early.

What a treadmill I was on. By doctors orders, I took a sleeping pill at night to help get through the night, and an antidepressant in the morning to help get through the day. That night, the cycle started all over.

While others in the house slept soundly, I vividly recall lying awake for hours. Sleep wouldn't come. I wondered if life would ever be normal for me again.

14. Agitation.

Agitation is a constant companion to the depressed person. It is a feeling of being disturbed and upset, and it never lets up. The depressed psalmist expressed it, "I am upset and disturbed. My mind is filled with apprehension and with gloom" (Psalm 6:3, TLB).

Even when there is apparently nothing triggering it, it is there. Depression itself is the cause. Rest and relaxation appear as unattainable desires.

I normally have no difficulty sleeping. If I do, I can at least lie still and rest. Not so when I was depressed. This inner agitation would not permit it. After twisting and turning to my mind's demands, I was forced to get up. I remember the many miles and hours I walked in my house during the night: up the hall, through the living room, the dining room, the kitchen, and back through the hall, wringing my hands with every step. Finally, I would return to bed hoping it would be different. It seldom was. Why? I was depressed and agitation is its companion.

15. Crying.

The depressed person cries a great deal. Everything appears in such dark gloomy shades that crying comes easily both day and night.

I know the experience of the psalmist, "Every night my pillow is wet with my tears" (Psalm 6:6, TLB). Tears occupied most of my time alone, but was not confined to being alone. I could hardly talk with anyone without crying, especially family members and close friends. I would telephone one of my children vowing I was not going to cry, but seldom succeeded. This always upset me, and certainly them, but it seemed out of my control. The tears just came...and came...and came.

16. Spiritual Alienation.

I felt spiritually out of touch. Even though I knew it was not true, I could not dispel the feeling that God had forsaken me and deservedly so. After all, I felt guilty about any and everything.

The spiritual disciplines, which normally filled me with joy and delight, came very hard. The feeling of spiritual alienation combined with other symptoms: withdrawal, guilt, agitation, etc., made attending church a real ordeal. My desire to pray and read my Bible waned. When I forced myself to do so, it seemed void of any real meaning or comfort.

17. Isolation.

When I was with friends, and even my family, I had this strange feeling I didn't belong. It was a feeling of detachment and isolation. This was increasingly frightful. I wondered if this meant I was beginning to lose touch with my surroundings. Thankfully, it did not prove to be so, but entertaining the possibility added to my anxiety and agitation.

18. Memory Loss and Forgetfulness.

Depression produces forgetfulness. I had great difficulty remembering immediate things. Did I take my medication or not? I couldn't remember. The memory loss is frustrating. I spent hours each day searching for things I needed but could not remember where I had put them. Any normal memory difficulty is worsened by depression.

You can easily see how this intensifies the great feeling of inadequacy you already have, thus making your depression more severe. It becomes a vicious cycle.

19. Eating Irregularities.

Like sleep, your eating may be affected either way. Some depressed persons lose their appetite, others overeat.

I could not eat. The very smell of food or thought of having to eat made me nauseous. What little I did eat, I forced down. In two months I lost 25 pounds. My ribs protruded so, I was ashamed to wear a bathing suit.

Depression may be a sure way to lose weight, surpassing most diet plans. Yet, I don't recommend it. No trim waist is worth the pain of depression.

20. Feeling of Losing Control.

I thought I was increasingly losing control of my abilities and life in general. I wondered how soon it would be before I was unable to care for myself, to attend to my personal and financial matters. This added even more to my mountain of anxiety.

Often this mental image oppressed my mind: I envisioned myself being carried down a river by a roaring current to a disastrous waterfall. Its speed and power were overpowering. I was being taken where I didn't want to go, to certain destruction. I fought frantically to gain control, but every limb or rock I grabbed was quickly torn from my grasp by the raging current. I saw myself as the victim of a turbulent force which was increasingly robbing me of the control of my life, and ultimately my life.

21. Loss of Interest in Personal Appearance.

Depressed women quit using makeup and men quit shaving. Uncombed hair and grubby clothes become standard. Generally, personal appearance ceases to be important to the depressed.

22. Diminished Sexual Desire.

It is common for the depressed person, both male and female, to lose interest in sex. This can cause a problem in a marriage relationship. The spouse of a depressed person may become very frustrated and experience feelings of rejection. Little does the spouse understand the cause is depression, not a lessening of love and commitment. The depressed person may be equally puzzled by this change in sexual desire, and would have great difficulty explaining it to his wife if he did understand.

23. Loss of Concentration.

Concentration becomes very difficult for the depressed person. Any responsibilities involving mental acuteness, alertness, competence, and clear thinking become laborious, if not impossible. Depression quenches creativity.

At the time I became clinically depressed, I was syndicating a weekly newspaper column. Writing my column, which normally I enjoyed, became a stressful burden, a real traumatic experience. It took me days to do what before had taken only a few hours.

24. Lack of Energy.

The depressed person experiences a feeling of general weakness and constant tiredness. It is there upon waking up and remains all day. Family physicians reveal the most common complaint of patients who are depressed and don't know what is wrong, is physical exhaustion and lack of energy.

I knew that working in the yard would be good for me, perhaps give me at least temporary relief from my troubled and tortured mind. But how could I cut grass for two hours with a power push mower, when I didn't even have the energy to walk to the shed to get out the mower. Everything I did, I had to force myself to do. Even then, it was a drag. This dilemma intensifies other symptoms.

25. Hopelessness.

At first the depressed person feels this strange horrible condition is temporary and he will soon get over it. As the symptoms become prolonged and more intense, hope begins to diminish. Hopelessness becomes the by-product and culmination of all the other symptoms combined.

Hopelessness is a growing conviction of the depressed person that his present state (this living hell of depression) has become his permanent state. He has become persuaded that things are never going to be any better, neither he nor his life will ever be normal again.

Hopelessness is the most dangerous symptom of all. It often becomes the prelude to suicide. With hope gone, he begins to feel that whatever death entails, it will be better than his present life. Death becomes more and more attractive as it is increasingly viewed by the depressed person as the only solution to his own living hell and the horror he is causing his family.

Hopelessness will likely produce suicidal thoughts and a death wish in every depressed person. Not everyone, however, will attempt suicide. But, it is extremely difficult even for professionals to predict which one will. That is why every depressed person manifesting hopelessness must be considered a potential suicide.

Though suicidal thoughts did come to my mind, I never did entertain them seriously. This I contribute to the grace of God and my family consistently assuring me they needed me. I did have a real death wish, but I wanted God to take my life rather than me do it. How glad and grateful I am now He didn't answer that prayer.

Hopelessness is also critical because it renders recovery more difficult. Any depressed person is more likely to overcome his depression if he can hold on to hope and expectancy of recovery even if he has no idea how or when.

If hopelessness is not the jumping off place, it is only a short distance away. So the depressed person and those seeking to help him, should make every possible effort to keep hope alive. Hope is the breath of the depressed. Where there is hope, there is life.

CONCLUSION

Well, this is what life is like in the world of the depressed. This may not be an exhaustive list of depression's symptoms. But surely it is enough to confirm the view of the depressed and convince the non-depressed that depression truly is a living hell!

Read on. There is good news. *You can overcome depression!* By God's help, I did. So can you.

— 10

Therapy for Depression

The good news is depression is a treatable illness. Not only treatable, but successfully so. Help is available.

Sometimes in its mildest forms, a person's depression may improve and even go away. Just as he doesn't know what caused it, neither does he know what got him over it.

Most depression, however, does not just go away. Depression is not something you can just "snap out of" no matter how earnest the desire. The depressed person needs to come to grips with his need and seek the appropriate help.

OVERCOMING THE RELUCTANCE

The sad news is many depressed persons never seek any kind of help.

I can understand this reluctance because I experienced it. I vividly remember the raging conflict within me. I was sick, knew that I was, and that I was getting worse and not better. Yet, I strongly resisted going for help. After all, I had never heard of a person being honored or receiving an award for being depressed. The commonly held view toward depression — that it is incorrect seems to make little difference — causes a depressed person to feel ashamed. Ashamed to have let the wheels run off his life and the inability to get them on again himself.

I was gripped with fear. When I was in my teens, my father had been hospitalized for depression. His being treated with electroshock therapy without benefit of anesthesia (as was practiced in the 1940's) was horribly etched in my mind. I not only assumed but was convinced this was what they would do to me. Even though I knew anesthesia now is used, I wanted no part of shock therapy.

The encouragement of my wife and children had not been able to break down my resistance until one morning our eldest son came to our home. He and my wife stood beside me as I sat in my bedroom. "Dad," he said, "we can't stand to see you hurt like this any longer. We are taking you to your doctor."

Sometimes a family has to do what a loved one needs them to do, not what he wants them to do. This is called tough love. How grateful I am my family loved me that much.

I knew they were right. I finally came to grips with the fact I had no other choice if I wanted to ever live normally again. With my consent, within a few hours we were in the office of my internist of 22 years. He caringly told me I needed the care of a psychiatrist, just what I feared he would say. Little did I ever dream that I would someday be on the other side of the therapist-patient relationship. Again I knew I was being told the truth. Hesitantly, I consented and sat in his examining room deep in thought and weeping as his staff arranged for my appointment with a psychiatrist. My emotions were mixed: sad and anxious for what I thought lay ahead, but yet the first sense of relief I had experienced in months because I had finally taken a positive step to get professional help.

This unwillingness of many depressed persons to go for help, especially men because of the male ego, has a number of causes: not knowing depression is their problem; thinking it will get better on its own; the stigma attached to depression and being treated by a psychiatrist or psychologist; lack of knowledge about available therapy; cost of therapy; and fear of various forms of therapy primarily due to stories they have heard of others when therapy was less advanced.

Whatever the reason, this reluctance to seek help desperately needs to be overcome. Any other choice requires too high a cost: the horrors of depression becoming a way of life, impaired family and interpersonal relationships, inability to work and function normally, and the possibility of suicide.

The general public is now far more enlightened and understanding of depression. Yet, the stigma attached to depression does still exist in some segments of our society, notably in the political arena and the work place. Prior treatment for depression is often used as a political weapon to defeat many capable candidates. There are still those who toss aside any job application where the person has been honest enough to acknowledge previous depression treatment. Even the common use of this question on job applications confirms the stigma is still alive and kicking.

The continued presence of this primitive and ignorant attitude is indeed unfortunate for depressed persons and their families. It deprives society of the benefits many have to offer. Science confirms the IQ, aptitudes, and creativity of most persons who have experienced depression are exceptionally high. History proves many of the world's most ingenious inventions and creative artistic achievements come from those who also suffered from depression. Two of the world's greatest leaders and statesmen, Abraham Lincoln and Winston Churchill, suffered from depression, yet gave outstanding leadership to their country in turbulent times. Personally, I had much rather have a public official or worker serving me who has acknowledged his need, gotten help, and overcome his depression than those who perpetuate their sickness by seeking to hide it from themselves and others.

Unfortunately, this stigma is still a possibility for any person who seeks treatment for depression. But, it is a risk that must be taken. No depressed person should assign himself to a continuing living hell simply because of the possible ignorant attitude of others. He must not let the problem of others (ignorance), prevent him from becoming free of his problem (depression).

KINDS OF THERAPY

There are various kinds of help available to the depressed person. The level of therapy needed will depend on the intensity and length of time of the depression. I will identify and help you understand the major forms of therapy.

1. Talking With a Non-Psychiatric Professional.
Often a person experiencing mild or non-clinical depression can be helped by talking to someone with whom he has a trust relationship. This may be a family member or very close friend with whom he feels free to share his thoughts and feelings. It may be a pastor, teacher, or family physician. I am not suggesting these are non-professionals, but rather non-psychiatric professionals.

To be helpful, the friend does not need to be an "expert" on depression. If it is someone with whom he feels free to honestly share his thoughts and feelings, and the friend has a listening ear, a caring heart, and a non-judgmental attitude, talk-time shared can be very helpful. If the friend has overcome depression himself, or has some understanding of it, the greater his ability to help. One of the purposes of this book is to enable every person to be that kind of friend.

2. Psychotherapy.
In plain language "psychotherapy" simply means talk therapy. It is give and take, mostly give, conversation with a person professionally trained in treating persons with mental and emotional impairments or problems. Such persons may be psychiatrists, psychologists, psychiatric nurses or psychiatric social workers.

It is important to know the difference between a psychiatrist and a psychologist. A psychiatrist is a fully trained medical doctor who has in addition completed a residency in psychiatry and specializes in the treatment of mental and emotional disorders. As a physician, he is able to prescribe medications. A psychologist is educated and trained in psychology, usually with a graduate degree, who also treats those with mental and emotional needs. Since the psychologist is not a physician, he is not permitted to prescribe medications, but relies primarily on psychological testing and psychotherapy for diagnosis and treatment. Sometimes a psychiatrist and psychologist will work together.

Psychotherapy is usually received as an outpatient, but can also be part of treatment during hospitalization. It tends to be rather long-term and expensive, depending on the severity of the depression. Some cities or counties have mental health centers or clinics staffed by professionals offering treatment for depressives on an "able to pay basis," reducing the cost.

While it is certainly beneficial in many areas, professionals themselves have recently acknowledged psychotherapy alone has historically proven not very effective in treating depression. The experience of many depressed patients confirms this view.

The current form of drug-free psychotherapy that appears to have the most success in treating depression is called Cognitive Therapy or the New Mood Therapy. It was developed at the University of Pennsylvania School of Medicine by Aaron T. Beck, M.D., and David Burns, M.D., and now practiced in most areas of the country.

3. Drug Therapy.

Great strides were made in the mid-1950's with the discovery and development of antidepressant drugs. This, perhaps more than any one thing, moved depression treatment out of the dark ages.

Most psychiatrists rely primarily on drug therapy to treat depressives. Many believe a combination of drug therapy and psychotherapy is the most effective. This tends to confirm my view expressed in Chapter 6 on Kinds of Depression. Whether depression begins organically or psychologically, if it remains undiagnosed and untreated long enough it will become both and both must be treated.

Most of us know little about antidepressants and approach them with uncertainty and anxiety. Being neither a physician nor a pharmacist, I do not have the knowledge or experience to deal with this subject in-depth. Hopefully I can help you understand enough about antidepressants and how they work to dispel some of the mystery and fear surrounding them.

First, you need to understand the chemical imbalance in the brain linked with depression. The brain contains substances called "amines." To be specific, three amines are identified: norepinephrine, dopamine, and serotonim.

These are chemical transmitters which the brain uses to send messages from one nerve to another. A nerve in our brain is not one continuous segment, but rather a series of disconnected segments. A brain message, vital to our normal functioning and well-being, passes through one segment of the nerve. When it reaches the end of that segment, it is transported to the next appropriate nerve segment by a chemical messenger, an amine.

You can readily see how important amines are. Well, it is here that the problem arises. One feature of any one unit (molecule) of this chemical messenger (amine) is that it only functions one time. When it has transported a brain message from one nerve ending to the next, it is then excreted from the brain and body as waste matter. Therefore, your brain needs an abundance of individual units of amines. For example: if amines were postmen, you would need 365 to get your mail every day of one year, not just one delivering your mail 365 times.

When the chemical imbalance related to depression occurs, one of two conditions exists: There are too few chemical units of amines, or the ones there have become impotent. Either of these conditions prevents the brain from functioning normally.

The problem is further complicated by the fact that at the present there is no laboratory test that accurately and conclusively determines whether there is a chemical imbalance. So even if one is suspected, there is no laboratory way to conclusively determine which of the two conditions exists: too few or impotent.

Enter antidepressants. These drugs correct either of these two conditions and balance the brain chemistry. There are three major groups of antidepressants: Tricylics, which energize and increase the potency of the amines; Monoamine Oxidase Inhibitors, which increase the quantity of amines; and the Serotonin Specific Uptake Inhibitors, such as Prozac, Paxil, and Zoloft, which are the most widely used.

Within each of these types of antidepressants there are numerous different drugs. Thus, prescribing and taking antidepressants, except for the experience of the physician, is largely a matter of trial and error. One that works for one person may not help another and vice versa. The crucial task is finding the right one for you.

I took five different prescribed antidepressants before finding one that helped. Three of them I very quickly realized my body could not tolerate. One I could tolerate, but it did nothing to help my depression and in my opinion made it worse. The fifth one did in time help.

Because there are so many different ones, and because it takes approximately 21 days for most antidepressants to produce discernible improvement, this can be quite time-consuming as well as costly.

Antidepressant drugs, even the one you find effective, may have some side effects for some individuals. Some of the more serious possible side effects may be: allergic reactions; muscle weakness; dizziness; confusion; fast, slow, or irregular heartbeat; and unusual bleeding. Some of the annoying but less serious possible side effects may be: loss of appetite; nausea; constipation; dry mouth; sexual problems; tremors; mild weakness; unusual unpleasant dreams; and loss of sleep. Newer and improved drugs with less side effects continue to be discovered.

Lithium, the drug of choice for bipolar manic depressive disorder (a mental impairment probably due to chemical imbalance in which periods of manic excitation alternate with melancholic depression), is usually very effective, but may cause some serious toxic effects. Thus, lithium levels need to be closely monitored through lab tests.

Most physicians do not view antidepressants as addictive drugs.

Taking antidepressants seems to bother some Christians who consider it a breach of their faith or commitment. This is, in my view, totally unfounded. The same person probably would not be bothered by taking insulin for diabetes. What is the difference between taking medication to correct a chemical imbalance in the brain and one to correct an insulin imbalance in the pancreas? If you are willing to take any medication at all — and certainly a Christian should be — there is no reason to exclude antidepressants.

My advice to a depressed person is to take antidepressants if all indications seem to confirm chemical imbalance has become linked with your depression. The proper drug is the quickest and most effective way to regain your chemical balance.

Yet, I do advise some caution. Unless the depression has become clinical, meaning you are unable to function, I would not take them without first trying other forms of therapy. Your depression may not be chemically involved and thus the drugs are unneeded. My personal experience, and that of others, has persuaded me that taking an antidepressant that proves unsuitable for you, may intensify certain aspects of your depression. I feel rather confident this happened to me.

If other forms of therapy have not enabled you to overcome your depression, I would advise you to take antidepressants. For reasons already stated, I do think it wise to have them prescribed by a psychiatrist or a physician who has a great deal of experience in treating depressives. The experience of the prescribing physician is even more crucial because of the absence of available conclusive laboratory tests.

Following recovery from the immediate depression, most psychiatrists prescribe a maintenance dosage for approximately one year in an effort to prevent a recurrence.

Fortunately, there are some natural antidepressants: herbal and nutrient alternatives to antidepressant drugs. Numerous research studies show them to work as well as the drugs and with much fewer side effects. Like drugs, they may require three to four weeks to be effective, and may work for some persons and not for others.

These natural antidepressants should not be taken at the same time as antidepressant drugs. If, however, you are not taking any drug, you may wish to consult your physician and your herbal/nutrient store consultant about taking a natural alternative. You may be able to improve your brain chemistry, help your depression, and avoid the side effects of the drugs.

4. Electroshock Therapy.

The medical name is electroconvulsive therapy (ECT). Prior to the discovery of antidepressants, ECT was used a great deal in the treatment of depression. Since then, however, it is used by most psychiatrists only as a last resort, only after everything else has failed.

As unpleasant as it may sound, ECT is usually quite effective when other forms of secular treatment have not been. As far as I have been able to discover, medical science does not understand exactly why it works, but acknowledges that it does.

ECT is administered by a psychiatrist. The patient is given a general anesthetic, electrodes are attached, and a measured amount of electrical current causes the body to convulse. Of course, the anesthetized patient is unaware of the convulsion. Much of the negative reputation of ECT comes from the days when the patient was not anesthetized but simply strapped down and knocked out by the convulsion itself. Thankfully, ECT has certainly become a lot more humane.

ECT is usually given in a series of 10 to 15 treatments depending on the severity and duration of the depression. It may be received during hospitalization or as an outpatient.

I am not aware of any serious side effects, but again let me remind you, I am not a physician. After awaking from the anesthetic, the patient is confused and disoriented, but this usually clears in a few hours. The worst side effect I am aware of is a rather severe memory lost. Most of the memory will eventually return, but I have observed it does not seem to do so completely.

Gratefully, ECT did get my father over his depression when nothing else did. This was prior to the advent of antidepressants. I would consent to ECT for myself or a family member only if all other forms of therapy had been adequately tried and failed. If that were my only hope to prevent remaining in the living hell of depression for the rest of my life, I would welcome it. I know of nothing worse than living in clinical depression, nothing. But how grateful I am to God that I did not have to resort to this last resort.

5. Spiritual Therapy.

Though it may not be recognized or acknowledged by all therapists, there is another form of therapy — spiritual therapy. I believe it is the only form of therapy that offers *complete* and *lasting* recovery from depression. Most secular therapists do not even think in terms of "lasting" or permanent overcoming of depression. When my psychiatrist first prescribed antidepressants, I asked how long I would need to take them. His response was I would need to take them until I recovered and then for at least a year longer *because my depression would probably return.* Apparently this is the most accepted medical view and the expectation of pharmaceutical companies. That was not good news. Rather the kind of news that could make a depressed person even more depressed.

I recognize with appreciation secular therapy. I finally availed myself of its help and would not discourage anyone from doing so. The two psychiatrists I saw, the antidepressants I took, and the one-week hospitalization on the psychiatric unit with its battery of physical tests, group and vocational therapy, were beneficial. The antidepressants improved the balance of my brain chemistry. All of this certainly kept me from getting worse. But none of this enabled me to be *completely* free of my depression. Life was better but not good, less miserable but not normal. I was still depressed, experiencing most of the same symptoms.

I also tried all of the practical suggestions for depression: I walked several miles everyday; ate healthy foods, what little I ate; took vitamin supplements, particularly the stress fighters C and B-complex; tried to rest and relax, which is not easy for a depressed person; and made sure I did something everyday to help other people. Even though these are good habits for anyone's well-being and may help with mild depression, I discovered they are not sufficient and have little effect on major and/or clinical depression.

I sought the help of several spiritual counselors I knew and respected only to discover they knew and understood essentially nothing about depression — a situation I pray this book will help correct. It was obvious they cared, but praying with me was all they knew to offer. I certainly value prayer and never underestimate its possibilities. But unless I was miraculously healed, I needed more than prayer and so does every depressed person.

In the midst of my confusion and searching, I became certain of one thing — the answer and solution to my need was in God. But why couldn't I find it? Where was the handle? How could I get hold of it?

I cried out to God to show me how to overcome this horrible depression. It wasn't the first time. Now my cry was more desperate. I realized I was fighting for my life.

God answered my prayer. Over time, piece by piece, He began to reveal to me insights about depression, spiritual truths and exercises, if accepted and appropriated, would enable me to overcome my depression.

As I was faithful to His guidance, He enabled me to overcome my depression. Since 1986 I have been free of abnormal depression relying on spiritual therapy and without any antidepressant drugs or secular therapy.

As I have shared through seminars these spiritual insights and exercises with others, many depressed persons who have appropriated them, have also been able to overcome their depression. To God be all the praise and glory!

CONCLUSION

If you have leaks in your roof, you have three options: First, you can do nothing. This will result in the situation getting worse until your carpet, furniture, and the house itself are ruined. Second, you can put buckets on the floor to catch the water when it rains. This will keep from ruining things, but does restrict your life-style. You can't fully use the room as it was designed because of the buckets. Plus, you have to keep emptying the buckets. This means you can't leave home for long to do the things you enjoy because it may rain and the buckets overflow. Third, you can fix the leaks. This may require more effort initially, but since it is the only option that really fixes the problem, it is your only wise choice.

This is a good illustration of seeking to fix depression. You can do nothing, allow it to keep getting worse until all is ruined. You can avail yourself of secular therapy. You may need to do this before you are able to fix the roof. In my experience and observation, however, secular therapy is in some ways like using the "buckets." It's far superior to doing nothing. It helps and prevents it from getting worse, but does not really fix the problem. You have to keep emptying the buckets, meaning you have to depend on the resumption and possible continuation of the therapy every time it "rains" (your depression occurs). I have noticed very few patients of therapists are ever permanently discharged.

I have concluded the most obvious and wisest choice of therapy for the depressed person is spiritual therapy. This is your best opportunity to fix the problem.

Let me emphasize again that if a chemical imbalance has become a part of your depression, drug therapy will probably be necessary before spiritual therapy can be fully appropriated. When a chemical imbalance exists in the brain, a person's ability to think, reason, understand, and appropriate truth to practice is impaired.

So any depressed person may need both secular and spiritual therapy. This would depend on whether the depression has become both organic and psychological and its severity. No program of treatment, however, should ever exclude spiritual therapy regardless of the severity. It is a must to *fix* it.

THE REST OF THE BOOK

The remainder of this book is devoted to sharing what God shared with me. I call this spiritual therapy. I believe with all my heart what God did for me, He can do for any depressed person who is willing to appropriate it. This conviction focuses my ministry on the UNDERSTANDING, PREVENTING, AND OVERCOMING DEPRESSION seminars and this book.

The Real Cause of Depression

In Chapter 8 on triggers, I identified four situations often linked with depression: a major loss; being betrayed, wronged, or rejected; bad decisions; and major disappointments. I called them "triggers" of depression.

If you are a close observer, you know I did not actually say these *caused* depression. This is what I wrote: "Frequently depression develops when one or more of the following circumstances have occurred or exists in a person's life."

No, I am not trying to trick you. I am making a point. That point is the first principle the Lord taught me in answer to my desperate cry for help.

Statistically about one out of every nine persons will experience clinical depression sometime during his life. This means about 90% of the population will never experience clinical depression.

Now consider this: Since these four situations are linked to depression, obviously approximately 10% of the population will experience one or more (probably all four) of them in their life. If these four things were the real cause of depression, then logic tells us the remaining 90% of the population *never experience* any losses, betrayals, bad decisions, or major disappointments.

Experience and observation clearly reveal this is not the case. Surely everyone, not just the 10% who become depressed, has one or probably all of these four situations occur in their life. If 100% experience these things but 90% never become depressed, then obviously these four situations are not the cause of depression. They may be the stimuli that spark its appearance, but losses, betrayals, bad decisions, and disappointments *do not cause* depression.

Then what is the real cause of depression? The Lord was impressing me with the necessity of knowing this if I was to begin to overcome my depression.

The real cause of psychological depression does not focus on what happens to us in our life, but how we react to what happens. The 10/90 ratio plainly reveals we do not all react alike. Why? Many reasons, but one in particular, the difference in our temperaments.

Depression is a matter of *perception*, the Lord kept revealing to me. Yes! Clearer and clearer it became. Depression *is* a matter of perception. "Lord, what does perception mean?" I asked. He gave me the answer. Perception is the way you see things to be.

This helps explain our differing reactions: we do not all view losses, betrayals, bad decisions, or major disappointments the same. One person sees them one way, another person a different way. Even the same person will have a different perspective at different times of the same or similar event.

Why do you have a wrong perspective? Because of faulty thinking. Thus, the bottom line: *the real cause of psychological depression is faulty thinking.* Your thinking gets messed up.

THE WAY WE WORK

To understand how faulty thinking is the real cause of psychological depression, it is necessary to know something of the dynamics of human behavior.

Simply put, your behavior (actions) results from your emotions (feelings), your emotions result from your thinking (thoughts). What you think determines how you feel, and how you feel determines how you act.

The moment you have a certain thought and believe it, you

will immediately have a corresponding emotion. This emotion will in turn have a corresponding action.

Let's illustrate this. Imagine you are a woman and are to be picked up by a family member late at night outside your downtown office building in a large city. Your ride is a few minutes late and you are standing on the sidewalk alone. Suddenly you see a man dressed in dark work clothes, a cap, and carrying a wooden stick. He is one block away and walking toward you. The thought enters your mind: that man is going to harm me. As you begin to accept this thought, you experience a corresponding emotion. What is it? Fear. Because you are afraid and anxious, you act accordingly. You walk across the street where a small group of well-dressed people are standing outside a restaurant. You stand very near them pretending to be a part of their group, but your eyes are glued on the man across the street from whom you have fled in fear. Much to your chagrin you see him stop near where you had been standing, with his stick remove the water meter cover, read and record the meter reading in his book, and move on down the sidewalk. Your original thought proved to be untrue. Yet, when you thought it was true, it controlled your emotions and actions. You feared and fled.

This is the way humans function. Our thoughts, be they real or imaginary, initiate and determine what we feel and do. Understanding this, it is easy to see how very important our thinking is. So the key to how we act, is actually what we think.

Long before the behavioral scientists figured this out, Solomon, endowed by God with unique wisdom, had already written it: "For as he [a man] thinketh in his heart, so is he" (Proverbs 23:7, KJV). When reading the Bible, substitute "mind" for "heart" and you will better grasp the meaning.

THE PROCESS OF FAULTY THINKING

The faulty mixed-up thinking that is the real cause of psychological depression does not occur in an instant. Rather it is a process that develops over time. Here is the faulty thinking process:

1. When you begin to feel depressed, your thoughts turn negative. This initial depressed feeling may be the normal depression all of us experience from losses that result from inevitable change. As you harbor, believe, and accept these negative thoughts, your thinking becomes increasingly negative. You are now unable to positively adjust to the loss and change, and your depression becomes abnormal. Now your thinking is dominated by negativity, causing your perception to become negative. You see and view all things pertaining to you in dark gloomy terms.

2. You become absolutely convinced that things really are as you perceive them to be. You do not entertain any possibility you could be wrong. You are certain the way you see and view everything pertaining to you is absolutely the way it is. It is truth; it is reality. No one can convince you otherwise.

As I was descending into the pit of clinical depression, I saw everything as negative with no hope of change. Here is one example:

In the spring of 1985, just a month before I hit the bottom of the pit, Alma and I moved from Charlotte, North Carolina, into my family home forty-five miles away in South Carolina following the death of my mother. Next door stood my grandfather's once grand Victorian house. It had been unoccupied for a couple of years and was showing the results. Inside were stored lots of unwanted furniture and things accumulated from family sources.

The old house next door occupied my thoughts night and day. They were all negative. I was absolutely convinced we could not find a buyer for the house. If we did, we couldn't sell it because we didn't have anything to do with all the things now stored in it.

This may not impress you as being a big issue and it doesn't me now, but you can believe it was of life and death importance to me then. Argue as artfully as they could, no one could convince me anything would work out with the old house. To me, there was no answer. I was convinced beyond doubt that my negative perception was the truth.

I wish you could see that old Victorian house now. A fine young couple bought it from us. This forced us to get it cleaned out. We had a yard sale, gave the rest to charity and that took care of that. The couple beautifully restored the house and it stands not only as a stately display of the past, but a constant reminder to me that what in depression we perceive as certain truth, may not be true at all. This leads us to the third step.

3. The negative thoughts that mix-up our thinking and feed our depression, always contain gross distortions. No matter how convinced we are that things really are as we perceive them to be, they usually are not. The negative perceptions of the depressed person are almost always perversions of reality. The Bible calls this "deception."

Not only does my grandfather's house prove this to me, but so do all the other things that I was convinced were real that turned out to be figments of my own negative thoughts and perception.

4. The steps in this process feed on each other and thus become a vicious cycle. The more negative our thinking becomes, the more distorted it becomes. The more distorted it becomes, the more negative it becomes. On and on the cycle goes, and with each cycle you slip deeper into the pit of depression.

NOT THE END OF THE STORY

As pessimistic as all this sounds, it really isn't. Rather, God was directing me to a fundamental truth that became my first ray of hope. Since depression is a matter of perception and is caused by faulty thinking, then if I can change the way I think and thus my perspective, then I can get out of this pit. I can overcome this horrible depression.

The only way to break the cycle and stop the process of faulty thinking is to change the way you think. This alone will change your perspective.

So, I knew what I had to do; I had to change my thinking. I didn't know how or when; I only knew if I was to ever be free of my depression, I had to do it.

Thank you, God, for good news that emerges out of the bad!

— 12 _____

Prerequisites for Overcoming Depression

In my struggle, God led me over a period of time to recognize nine prerequisites to overcoming depression. These nine principles are either truths to be accepted or actions to be taken.

I discovered complying with these nine principles will *not* free you from depression, but is essential and necessary to being in a position to become free.

After understanding and acknowledging that depression is a matter of perspective and caused by faulty thinking, the following steps position you to overcome depression:

1. Have a Complete Physical Examination.

One of the first things any person experiencing prolonged major depression should do is have a complete physical examination. This is to seek to determine whether you are suffering from organic or psychological depression, or both.

Tell your family physician or internist you are experiencing depression, and you would like for him to do all the tests or studies necessary to either confirm or eliminate any physical cause for your depression.

Some he may wish to include are the following: A review of any known physical problems you already have and the medications you are taking to see if they can produce depression as a side effect; blood tests for thyroid function, such as a T4, to test for hypo or low thyroid; a glucose tolerance test for possible low blood sugar; and a brain scan for a possible tumor, if other indications would warrant it. There may be other studies your physician will want to include.

In most instances this examination would probably be done as an outpatient. Since my depression had already reached the clinical level, I was admitted to the psychiatric unit of a general hospital for a week under the care of both my psychiatrist and internist. While the tests were being done, I was also receiving therapy for my depression: drug, psycho, group, and occupational.

The severity and duration of your depression would enable you and your physician to decide whether to have the studies done on an outpatient or hospitalized basis. Regardless of which, the studies do need to be done. You and your therapist need to know what kind of depression you are dealing with in order to know the treatment required.

2. Establish a Saving Relationship With Jesus Christ.

You do not have to be a Christian to be depressed, and I am surely not proposing you have to be a Christian to get better from your depression. But in my opinion, a person does need to be a Christian to experience *lasting* liberation from depression.

According to the Bible: all persons have sinned (Romans 3:23); are under the wages or penalty of sin, which is death (Romans 6:23); need to be saved; and this salvation is offered to every person through repentance of sin and faith and personal acceptance of Jesus Christ as Savior and Lord (Romans 5:8, John 3:16, 1 Corinthians 15:3-4, Romans 10:9, 13).

Every person has to come to grips with these three elements: his past, his present, and his future. Failure to do so will naturally and ultimately engulf life in a cloud of despair, anxiety, and depression for any normal and rational human being.

When a person becomes a Christian and thus the blood atonement of Jesus Christ is imputed to him, all three of these are instantly and eternally taken care of: His past is forgiven, all his sins are forgiven and forgotten by God. His present is provided for by the daily providential care of a loving Heavenly Father. His future is assured by God's promise of eternal life where "God shall wipe away all tears from their eyes; and there shall be no more death, neither sorrow, nor crying, neither shall there be any more pain; for the former things are passed away" (Revelation 21:4, KJV).

There is no other way to so effectively and assuredly take care of your past, present, and future.

Life is about living; depression is about existing. It is God's desire for every person to live abundantly, not just exist. But no person is really ready to live until he is prepared to die, and death is inevitable for all. Only the Christian has his past, present, and future positively taken care of.

The Apostle John expressed it this way: "He that hath the Son hath life; and he that hath not the Son of God hath not life" (1 John 5:12, KJV).

All I have been taught psychologically and theologically, all I have observed in others, and my own experiences convince me that only a Christian can be lastingly free from depression. Even so, what God has said in the Bible is the foundation of my conviction.

3. Possess a Firm Belief in the Sovereignty of God.

What we believe is important. How we react to the situations and circumstances that occur in our life is greatly determined by what we believe.

To deny there is a God, or to believe that He created everything then withdrew to let the world and all in it flap for themselves, leaves you with only one conclusion. That is to see yourself a victim in a wild random world over which you nor anyone else has any control. Despondency and depression are the logical consequences of such beliefs.

But to firmly believe God created all things, and continues to sovereignly govern and control all things according to His plan and purpose (which is based on His infinite and unchangeable love for those committed by faith to Him), enables you to react positively to life's events regardless of how bad they appear to be.

I thank God the physical cause of my voice impairment (laryngeal dystonia), is not life-threatening. Yet my response to having to give up my pastoral ministry because of it was devastating, and vastly contributed to my depression. In my struggle to get out of the pit of depression, God revealed that part of my faulty thinking was my "victim" complex.

He focused my attention on something I had always firmly believed, but in my faulty negative thinking had forgotten — the sovereignty of God.

I did not understand then, nor do I now, why I have this relatively rare voice impairment. But God restored my basic belief in the sovereignty of God. This enabled me to firmly believe and publicly declare that it could not have happened unless God allowed it, though He did not decree or cause it to happen; and that what God allows to happen in the life of a Christian, He has already planned and destined for His glory and our ultimate good.

My negative "victim" thinking began to change. My restored belief in His sovereignty began to change my reaction to what had happened to me. This helped position me to overcome my depression.

Our belief concerning the degree of God's involvement in our difficult circumstances surely impacts the way we respond and react. We become what we believe.

4. Align Yourself With God's Will.

Sin that is not confessed, repented of, and forgiven can and does cause depression. Therefore, if you have not dealt with past sin, or persist in doing that which is known sin, you are not in a position to overcome your depression.

The depressed person who continues to sin by living in an adulterous relationship, can take antidepressants till the pharmacists' shelves look like Old Mother Hubbard's cupboard, but he will not experience lasting freedom from depression. He may temporarily improve, but he will not get well and stay well.

Prerequisite to overcoming depression, is aligning yourself and your life with what you believe to be the will of God as it is revealed in His Word, the Bible. Then you have taken an essential step toward a position to enable you to overcome your depression.

INTERMISSION

This is heavy stuff. Let's take a break.

These first four prerequisites may or may not seem difficult to you, depending on your prior knowledge and experience with the Christian faith.

Also I need to serve you notice – the remaining five are difficult for everyone. They are principles that the depressed person must accept, believe, then act on.

Admittedly, for me they were traumatic. One by one God revealed these principles to me. The stronger the message became, the deeper I dug in my heels. I didn't even want to hear these things He was revealing, much less accept them.

He lovingly countered my resistance with a persistent question, "French, do you want to get well?" This shook me. This thought grabbed and held my attention.

My answer could only and always be "Yes!" But in saying it, I knew what it meant – I had to agree with the principles. They were progressive: meaning only after I wrestled and willingly agreed with one principle, did God reveal the next one to me. They are connected and one grows out of the previous one. Acceptance of one was necessary to even hear the next one.

Admitting to these difficult truths about myself and my depression, was indeed where the rubber hit the road. But He made it clear: it was the road that led out of depression.

So, let's continue:

5. Recognize and Accept the Fact Your Responses to Your Circumstances, Not Your Circumstances, Are the Real Causes of Your Psychological Depression.

There are some circumstances that occur in our life as a result of our own actions. Others occur over which we have no control. But in both cases we do control our response and reaction to the circumstance.

I sat on the porch of my home one afternoon deep in thought, struggling with this word that had come from God. The Holy Spirit pulled this experience from my memory.

A parishioner asked me to visit her neighbor who was diagnosed terminally ill. She thought I might be of some help to her, but as so often happened, I received the help and inspiration. When this attractive lady in her mid-30s met me at the door, I was surprised. She was joyful and happy, not morose and depressed as I had expected a person waiting to die to be. After introducing myself, she graciously invited me in. As we sat talking in her living room, her peace and joy became more evident. She picked up a book from the side table and handed it to me. "Have you ever read this book?" she asked.

After glancing at the title, *Man's Search for Meaning* by Viktor Frankl, I told her I had never seen it. "That book," she continued, "has changed my life. I want to give you this copy."

I sat enthralled as she shared the truths she had learned from the book: Everything can be taken from a person but the right to choose your attitude to any given circumstance that occurs in your life. This privilege is inalienable. "I can't control my illness or the death it may bring," she said, "but I do have the right and option to choose how I respond, what my attitude toward it will be. By God's grace I chose peace and joy, not sadness and despair." I thanked her, prayed with her, and rushed back to my study eager to discover more of this book that had so obviously impacted her life.

Twelve years later I am sitting on my porch struggling

desperately to find my way out of the pit of depression; remembering this experience caused me to relive not only the experience but the truth. It is not what happens to us in life, but our reaction to it that determines the quality of our life. During my ministry I had shared this book and its truth with many hurting people. Now I needed this truth, and through recall God had blazoned it upon my mind again after I had lost hold of it.

It is prerequisite to liberation from depression to recognize and accept this truth: your response (attitude, thinking, and perception) to your circumstances, not your circumstances, is the real cause of your depression.

6. Stop Justifying Your Depression and Give Up Your Right to Be Depressed.

Most depressed persons readily come up with a list of reasons to justify their depression. They can point to numerous circumstances in their life, any one of which they consider bad enough to depress them and provide sufficient right to feel as they do.

Sometimes a counselor will help you claim this right. Both my psychologist and my psychiatrist, at whose request I shared some of the difficult things that had happened in my life, said to me, "French, no wonder you are depressed. You have had enough bad things happen to you to make you depressed."

On both occasions I emerged from their office feeling better. Still depressed, but feeling better. They both had given support to my justifying my depression, providing me with a sense of relief. Now it was all right for me to feel this way. By all my hard knocks, I had earned the right to be depressed. So I would just cast off all blame, and start searching for whatever there was in depression to enjoy.

An immediate problem here; it is very difficult to find any enjoyment in depression. Even if I could find any, which I didn't, that wasn't what I wanted. I didn't want to enjoy it, I wanted to get over it, to be free of it.

The world will allow you to justify your depression. It is not too encouraging, however, to realize this same world will also allow you to drink poison if you choose. Even so, all depressives tend to hold tightly to this right to justify. All humans feel better if we can blame all our problems on somebody or something other than ourselves.

God invaded my thoughts. He would allow me to be depressed, but He would not allow me, nor any Christian, to justify my psychological depression or claim it as a right because of hard knocks. Through Jesus Christ's life, death, and resurrection, God has already provided a Christian with everything needed to prevent it from happening. So why should He allow me to justify it? To do so would in itself be a denial of truth.

Frankly, I did not want to hear this, but God made it clear. If I wanted to be free of my depression, I not only had to hear, I had to accept this truth. I must stop justifying my depression and give up my right to be depressed. This is a must for every psychologically depressed person who wants to overcome his depression.

This is not to deny the stress and hurt that accompanies tragic events and bad circumstances in a person's life. They do hurt. I have known some persons into whose life not just a little rain fell, but a flood of unbelievably bad events occurred. But if 90% of the persons who have such circumstances in their life do not become clinically depressed, then there is no way for me to justify my depression. If my response, not my circumstance, is the real cause of my depression, then I can claim no right to be depressed.

7. Assume the Responsibility and Accountability for Your Depression.

Accepting the previous principles confronted me with this truth: As much as it pained me to admit it, I was depressed because I had allowed it to happen.

I sensed this was coming from God, but I found it very difficult to accept. After all, being depressed was painful enough, without having to admit that it was my fault. Though it was a logical conclusion to be drawn from the previous truth I had accepted, I was still resisting. I just couldn't bring myself to accept the blame for my depression.

In the midst of this struggle, an event occurred that rendered me helpless to resist any longer. My otolaryncologist filled out the medical form requested annually by my Presbyterian Board of Pensions concerning my voice impairment. He enclosed a copy of his notes from my last examination, which was during the time I was depressed. Before forwarding them to the Board, I glanced over his notes. "French has allowed himself to become depressed," he wrote.

I was furious. Flames shot from my eyes and smoke poured from my ears. Not really, but I was angry enough for it to happen. I could not believe Jim, my friend, brother in Christ, and my doctor, could possibly be so cruel and insensitive. Did he not know I was hurting enough without being blamed for it all?

"Look at this," I said, handing Alma his notes. "Can you believe Jim has accused me of *allowing* myself to become depressed! I am going to telephone him right now and give him a piece of my mind." (This in spite of the fact, I was beginning to suspect there is a danger in giving others a piece of your mind. If you do this too often, you don't have much of your mind left.)

While stomping to the telephone to call this heartless doctor and release my anger, the Lord stopped me in my tracks. The Holy Spirit brought to my memory two verses of Scripture I had read privately and publicly hundreds of times. They are the words of Jesus: "Let not your heart be troubled, ye believe in God, believe also in Me" (John 14:1, KJV), and, "Let not your heart be troubled, neither let it be afraid" (John 14:27, KJV). The Holy Spirit taught quickly and deeply. There is no better description of depression than Jesus' words, a troubled and fearful mind ("heart" in the Bible is better understood if translated "mind"). So Jesus was saying to all who believe in God and Him, don't "let" (allow) this to happen to you.

I fell to my knees broken and sobbing. "Lord, Jim is right," I cried. "O Lord, it is the same thing You have been trying to get me to recognize and accept all this time. It is my fault. I have been depressed because I have *allowed* myself to be."

I could do nothing else. It is totally inconceivable that Jesus would tell me not to let it happen unless I had the ability to not allow it to happen. My knowledge of and faith in Jesus prevent me from believing He would tell me to do something I was totally incapable of doing.

This is not to suggest that a person would *choose* to be depressed. Choosing and allowing are not the same. Choosing is a conscious act, allowing may be an unconscious act as well as a conscious act. It is possible to allow something to happen that you do not necessarily choose to happen.

My resistance was gone. The truth was undeniable: psychological depression is something a person allows to occur. It was the hardest truth I had to accept, but there was nothing left for me to do. I accepted the responsibility and accountability for my depression. With this step, as difficult as it was, I took a giant step toward recovery.

8. Assume the Responsibility and Exert the Effort to Help Yourself Overcome Your Depression.

After I was finally able to acknowledge and admit I had allowed myself to become depressed and therefore must be accountable for it, I discovered something extremely helpful in this. Only after my admission was I able to see it.

Up until now I thought I was dependent on someone else to get me out of my depression. If I could just find the right person, the right therapist, the right doctor, then he would be able to get me out of this horrible pit. Since all of my efforts to find just this right person had failed, my hopes of recovery dimmed. Dimmed because the logical conclusion of my thinking was: if I can't find the right person, then I can't recover.

Now that I had discovered and admitted that *I* had gotten myself into this depression, then it dawned on me, by the prompting of God's Spirit, that *I* also had the capability of getting myself out. If I had gotten myself in, then I had the option to get myself out. This realization had a tremendous impact. It liberated me from seeing myself as a *victim* of depression.

As long as the depressed person denies any responsibility for getting himself in and out of depression (as almost all depressed persons do), then he can only conclude he is a victim of depression. As a victim, he sees himself having no control whatsoever over his becoming or overcoming depression. He sees himself as a victim of depression because of his circumstances, the actions of others, or some satanic force and therefore there is nothing he can do about it.

There are few things more damaging to the depressed person than this victim complex. It essentially means he is likely to stay in the pit of depression.

It is admitting you have allowed yourself to become depressed that positions you to accept the responsibility and exert the effort to get yourself well. Then accepting this responsibility and challenge, you are set free from any victim complex you may be holding onto so tightly.

When I assumed the responsibility and set out to help myself overcome my depression, I experienced a tremendous breakthrough. The victim complex was gone; the possibility of recovery had taken on new life.

9. Embrace Hope.

In my last pastorate I met on Wednesday mornings with a group of members for prayer and sharing. Our sharing became very personal. I recall one morning a lady saying sadly, "I don't believe I will ever be able to stop smoking."

After a few moments of silence in the group, I responded. "I think you are right, Mary, I don't believe you will ever stop smoking."

"Why, Pastor," she exclaimed, "that's not very encouraging. Why do you believe I will never be able to stop smoking?"

"Simply because *you* do not *believe* that you will. Unless you believe that it can happen, I doubt seriously that it ever will." I tried to speak the truth to her in love.

Now years later, in my struggle to be free from my depression, the Holy Spirit was speaking to me the truth I had spoken to her.

Embracing hope is prerequisite to and an essential part of overcoming anything, including depression. What does it mean to embrace hope? It means to believe that the recovery you so desperately want to occur will occur. It is to believe that your future state is going to be better than your present state. Hopelessness is to believe your present miserable state is going to be your permanent state. To embrace hope is to deal by faith a death blow to hopelessness.

To embrace hopelessness and despair is to consider God a historical figure only. To embrace hope is to believe God is today the same as He has always been and continues to extend His love, care, and power to all who call upon Him.

CONCLUSION

Your efforts to overcome your depression will succeed in direct relationship to the degree you are able to fulfill these nine prerequisites.

It was a struggle for me. It probably will be for you. It takes a lot of soul-searching and humility. Struggle with each of these truths as long as you have to. Strive until you can accept and agree with each one. These admissions must take place for you to be ready to overcome your depression.

In the next two chapters I will share with you the specific

things God told me to do to overcome my depression. He gave them to me only after I had struggled through to acceptance of each of these prerequisite truths and principles.

Let me make sure you understand. The content of the next chapters will be effective for overcoming your depression to the degree you are able to humbly and earnestly acknowledge, admit, and do the prerequisite truths.

— 13

Overcoming Depression: Changing Your Thinking

Since the real cause of psychological depression is faulty thinking, then it becomes obvious the way to overcome it is to change our thinking.

So far, simple enough. Now comes the hard question. How do we change our thinking?

Though some secular therapists agree with the need for the depressive to change his thinking, few offer any substantial help in telling us how we can change our thinking. Basically their advise is: you just do it. Just change it. Think positively.

As a depressed person, this offered me little guidance. If I could control my thinking and think positively, I probably would have never been depressed in the first place. My depressed state was evidence that I could not now of my own volition control or turn my thinking in any direction I chose.

Positive thinking founded on reality is valuable and therapeutic. But, if it is not based on reality, it is deception, not truth. It is like many of the old beach houses along the South Carolina coast where I live. They are built on sand with inadequate foundations. They may look very attractive, but when the high winds and water surges of the hurricanes come, they crumble and fall.

Positive thinking can be totally void of truth, and as such, is very destructive. Consider the person under the influence of drugs who "positively thinks" he can fly, but leaps to his death from a tall building because his perception of reality is distorted.

When I went to God with the question of how I was to change my thinking, the answer began to come. The principles I had accepted (previous chapter) had started me in the right direction. But, since I was still depressed, much of my thinking must still be confused and mixed-up even though it all seemed true to me. Apparently I had a long way to go in changing my thinking, so I cried out to Him, "O Lord, You have already helped me, but I need more. My thinking must still be mixed-up because I am still depressed. Please, Lord, show me how to change my thinking."

Deep down I knew the victory over my depression was to be found in God, but I had not been able to discover how. I could not get hold of what I was to do. I had prayed and begged God for an immediate victory and healing. I believed God could do that, yet it didn't happen.

He countered my disappointment by making it clear that I was to be involved in my healing. It would not come by sovereign decree as a miracle, rather through a self-involved spiritual process.

The answer to how do you change your thinking, gradually became known. The counterfeit is revealed by exposing it to the genuine. A synthetic diamond may be very attractive and deceive many, but when you place it beside a real diamond you discover it is not real at all.

As a depressed person my thoughts about myself and my circumstances were reality to me. I was convinced, as are all depressed persons, that everything was exactly as I perceived it to be. All my thoughts appeared real, a correct and true analysis of the way things were. This made changing my thoughts even more complicated.

First I had to discover which of my thoughts were distortions of the truth. To do this, my thoughts had to be exposed to the truth. This was the only way to determine whether they were true or false.

As long as there has been man there has existed the burning question: What is truth? Every person has to grapple with this question and arrive at a conclusion. Whether we do so consciously or not, everyone answers by the focus and direction of his life and the object of his highest devotion.

Years ago I had made that decision for myself and experienced its confirmation through the years. As a Christian believer, I accept the Bible, the Word of God, as the only infallible source and rule for my faith (what I believe) and my practice (what I do). I believe the one and only reality in this world is what God says, and the Bible is our revelation and record of God's words. That alone is truth.

I had unknowingly allowed my thinking to become faulty and distorted, because I had unintentionally departed from applying this conviction. What had happened to me, happens to every psychologically depressed person — *we replace (exchange) God's truth with Satan's lies.*

The Bible describes Satan (the devil) with these words: "He was a murderer from the beginning, and abode not in the truth, because there is no truth in him. When he speaketh a lie, he speaketh of his own: for he is a liar, and the father of it" (John 8:44, KJV). His desire and purpose toward every person is "to steal, and to kill, and to destroy" (John 10:10, KJV).

Since you may encounter this, let me warn you. There are a few preacher/teachers and their followers who believe depression is solely a matter of demon possession. Thus they conclude and practice that deliverance from the "demon of depression" is all that is needed to free one from depression. Their "ministry" to any depressed person is to cast out this demon.

Several times some Christians commanded the "demon of depression" to leave me. In my state of desperation and confusion, I welcomed any possibility of getting out of the pit. I was never aware of it being any help, though I was grateful for their care and concern.

I have known several persons who were ministered deliverance by someone holding to this view. Though some report a brief feeling of relief, in every case it made no significant or lasting contribution to their overcoming depression. This momentary feeling of relief was probably a placebo effect.

Anyone who really believes the Bible must acknowledge there is such a thing as demon possession, historically and currently, and there are rare occasions when exorcism is needed. I do not believe, however, that it is the sole reason for or answer to depression. Neither the Bible nor experience seems to support the "demon of depression" view. Remember Jesus expressed depressive feelings, and He was definitely not possessed of any demon.

Actually, this view and its practice is harmful to the depressed because it gives support to their victim complex. Also it shatters any hope they are desperately holding onto and deepens their depression. Why? Because what they were told is their only means to recovery has obviously failed since they are still depressed.

Surely, it is equally wrong to claim Satan has no part in depression. Without doubt, Satan is involved as he is in everything that seeks to steal, kill, and destroy us. In my opinion, his role here involves oppression, not possession. (This does not diminish the fact that the depressed person must still accept the responsibility and accountability for his psychological depression.) When we allow Satan to deceive us, we come under his oppression and he succeeds in getting us to unknowingly replace God's truth with his lies. Thus reality becomes distorted in our thinking. Distortion of reality is what depression is all about. Depression serves Satan's purposes well. There is no better way for him to steal, kill, and destroy a person's life, reducing it to a miserable existence void of hope, joy, peace, and purpose, than through depression.

With this revelation — that I had replaced God's truth with the devil's lies — the solution became evident. The procedure had to be reversed. I must knowingly replace the devil's lies with God's truth. The process by which this takes place involved spiritual exercises I was to do. This alone would change my thinking.

Logically all of the exercises He revealed to me involved the Bible, God's Word. There was no other way my thoughts could be exposed to reality since the Bible alone is truth and reality. It is the written revelation of Jesus Christ who is "the way, the truth, and the life" (John 14:6, KJV). This very Jesus declared "ye shall know the truth, and the truth shall make you free" (John 8:32, KJV).

Free from what? Free from bondage. Including the pit of depression? Yes! As I began to do the spiritual exercises each day, the truths I discovered, combined with the principles I had already accepted (previous chapter), my thinking started to change. I began to experience for the first time in months, some light in my world of darkness.

It didn't occur overnight. It took time. But I knew my thinking was changing, and because it was freedom from the pit of depression was at last a real possibility.

— 14

Overcoming Depression: Spiritual Exercises

Accepting the truths and principles God had revealed to me (Chapter 12), positioned me for healing. In accepting these truths, I had agreed:

1. That my response to my circumstances, not my circumstances, was the cause of my depression;

2. To stop justifying my depression and give up my right to be depressed;

3. That I was accountable for my depression because I had allowed it to happen;

4. To assume the responsibility for my own healing and exert the effort, by God's help, to make it happen.

It was obvious where God was leading me. My agreement to these truths committed me to having a part in my own healing. God could, of course, sovereignly do it without me. He does on occasion supernaturally heal people of all kinds of infirmities. But this was apparently not His plan for my depression. I believe in my case, and with most cases of depression, God considers it important for the person to be involved in his own healing.

One thing was for sure, searching for someone else to be my "healer," to get me completely out of my depression, had not worked. There was no doubt; God was pointing His finger at me. I was to be my own "healer."

This did not mean I was to do it all myself. How well I knew the impossibility of that. As in all things, I must rely on His guidance and power. This executed a biblical principle I discovered long ago: I can't do it without God; He won't do it without me. It is God's usual natural way of our receiving each of His gifts, whether it concerns salvation, the filling of His Spirit, or healing.

At that point I didn't know the what or how of my part, but He had brought me this far and I was willing to trust Him to carry me all the way. I had come too far to give up and turn back. Besides, there was no other place to go or route to take.

SPIRITUAL EXERCISES

When I have been willing to trust Him and walk by faith, God has never failed me. He didn't this time either. He began to reveal the "how" by showing me things I was to do faithfully and consistently each day using my Bible. They were identified in my mind as spiritual exercises.

Immediately I recognized I was no expert on spiritual exercises. Oh, I knew about, tried to practice, and had often preached on Bible reading, prayer, giving, and other Christian disciplines. But I sensed there was something more here I needed to understand.

I found these words of advice from the Apostle Paul to young Timothy: "Spend your time and energy in the exercise of keeping spiritually fit. Bodily exercise is all right, but spiritual exercise is much more important and is a tonic for all you do. So exercise yourself spiritually and practice being a better Christian, because that will help you not only now in this life, but in the next life too" (1 Timothy 4:7-8, TLB).

The concept God desired me to understand formed in my mind: A spiritual exercise is time and energy spent in improving our total well-being by focusing on that which pertains to our spiritual being.

With rare exceptions, depressed persons desperately want to get out of their pit of misery and pain. I surely did. Whatever time and energy it required, I was ready to devote to my healing. It was then God began to tell me specifically what I needed to do to get out of the pit.

1. STOP MAKING NEGATIVE STATEMENTS

The more depressed I became, the more negative my spoken words became. Practically every statement I made regarding myself or my circumstances was negative. I was constantly declaring, "I can't do anything right!...I am a failure at everything!...Nothing ever works out right for me!"

That Alma was able to survive living with me like this, is surely a testimony to the sufficiency of God's grace. I was sick of it myself. Who knows? Probably God was getting a little tired of me like this also. I knew how negative I was, but that was my perspective. All my negativism seemed exactly how things actually were, so how could I be truthful and say anything else.

In my mind God clearly revealed that if I wanted to overcome my depression, I must *stop making negative statements!*

As usual I argued with God. "How can I stop saying negative things, when that is how I think, that is what I see?" I soon understood He wasn't presently expecting me to be rid of my negative thoughts, just don't *speak* them. My thoughts would only change by doing the spiritual exercises. This would take time. But it was essential that I immediately stop verbalizing my negative thoughts.

I wondered why not speaking it was so important. Then He revealed to me this biblical principle: *The words we speak greatly affect and determine the quality of our life.* This is what I found in the Bible:

"If you want a happy good life, keep control of your tongue and guard your lips from telling lies" (1 Peter 3:10, TLB).

"A man's moral self shall be filled with the fruit of his mouth, and with the consequence of his words he must be satisfied [whether good or evil]. Death and life are in the power of the tongue, and they who indulge it shall eat the fruit of it [for death or life]" (Proverbs 18:20-21, AMP).

"The things that come out of the mouth come from the heart,

and these are the things that make a person ritually unclean" (Matthew 15:18, TEV).

There is no doubt. The Bible declares it and human experience confirms it: the words we speak greatly affect the quality of our life. The more we verbally declare a thought, the more deeply it becomes entrenched in our innermost being, permeating and affecting us in body, soul, and spirit. The person who declares over and over again, "I am so stupid. I can't do anything right," will eventually become practically dysfunctional regardless of his innate intelligence and skills.

Words spoken by others can also affect us. A child who is told repeatedly that he is dumb, will grow into adulthood believing himself to be dumb and thus acting dumb. Parents, please take heed.

Spoken words are powerful. They form, shape, and affect us even beyond our understanding. We cannot always control the words spoken to us by others, but we can, with concerted effort, control our own words. To stop making negative statements is wise for anyone. For one who wants to avoid or overcome depression, it is a must.

Now what is a negative statement? I wasn't sure. I told God if I was to stop making negative statements, I had to better understand what they were.

The confusion began to clear. A negative statement is not a true statement that involves an undesirable condition. My youngest grandchild broke his leg. When he said, "Granddaddy, I fell and broke my leg," he was not making a negative statement. He was telling the truth. It was reality. For him to say as he drags his heavy cast along the floor, "My leg is not broken," is not a positive statement. That is a denial of reality and there is nothing positive about it.

What then is a negative statement? There are two ways I can make a negative statement. First, if I verbalize a negative thought or opinion about myself, my abilities, my actions, or my circumstances, I make a negative statement. "I can't do anything right. I am a total failure in every aspect of my life." These are negative statements. Obviously, practically everything coming from my mouth was a negative statement.

Second, if I verbally predict a negative outcome concerning a situation in my life in which the outcome has not yet been determined, I have made a negative statement. If after reading in the church bulletin an invitation to go snow skiing, I say to a friend, "I would like to go skiing with the group, but I know if I do I would break my leg." A woman taking a shower discovers a lump in her breast. Alarmed and frightened she bounds out of the shower, rushes to the telephone, and with panic tells her husband, "I have breast cancer!" These are two illustrations of negative statements. Both are verbalized negative predictions regarding circumstances whose outcomes have not yet been determined. I have not been on the ski trip, nor has the woman consulted a physician. Yet both of us have already verbally declared a negative outcome as truth, even though the real outcome has not been determined.

If I am to stop verbalizing my negative thoughts, then what will I do with them? There is no profit in playing games with myself. I can't pretend these negative thoughts are not present. They not only flash through my mind like the scenes of a movie, but they often dwell there and I can't get rid of them. This is the life of the depressed. This is his world.

God convinced me He understood. He again confirmed that for now, He was not expecting that I not have the thought, just don't speak it. He would show me what to do with these negative thoughts. His answer was the beginning of the specific spiritual exercises.

THE FIRST SPIRITUAL EXERCISE

Few tools are needed for these exercises. You only need a Bible (I suggest one of the modern translations such as The

Living Bible because it is easier to understand and personalize), a composition book (use a new one so it can be used exclusively for your spiritual exercises), a pen, and a minimum of 30 minutes each day. The more time you devote each day, the quicker your thinking will change. This is a small price to pay for preventing or overcoming depression. Anyone who has been depressed or threatened with it would gladly give this and more.

This first spiritual exercise deals with what I am to do with those negative thoughts I still have but am not to verbalize. It enables me to heed the exhortation of God through the Apostle Paul, "For the weapons of our warfare are not carnal, but mighty through God to the pulling down of strong holds. Casting down imaginations, and every high thing that exalteth itself against the knowledge of God, and *bringing into captivity every thought to the obedience of Christ*" (2 Corinthians 10:4-5, KJV).

This is how God taught me to do this. Instead of verbalizing a negative thought when it comes to mind, you write it in your notebook under a page headed, "Testing the Thought." Preface it with the words, "My Thought." Carefully leave blank lines after each statement you write. Do not be concerned if for a while your pages contain only negative statements and blank spaces. Because as you read the Scriptures (as prescribed in the second spiritual exercise we will discuss later), God will reveal to you specific Scripture verses that will expose each of your negative statements for what they are — lies! Now write this Scripture verse God's Spirit has enabled you to discover in the blank lines under the negative statement it refutes. Preface the verse with the words, "Reality (God's Truth)." (See APPENDIX TWO for an example of this exercise.) This is vital: Each day, for as many statements as you have found answers, read *silently* your thought, then read *aloud* God's answer.

As you diligently and faithfully do these spiritual exercises you will make the same discovery I did. God will provide a response verse to every one of your negative statements. God's truth will refute and reveal the distorted nature of your thoughts. Previously you have in your thoughts unknowingly replaced God's truth with Satan's lies, believing the lies to be the truth. This is the essence of depression. This is why you are depressed.

Through this exercise, as you test each negative statement and by God's truth take it captive, a process is taking place. *Your thoughts are being changed.* The faulty thought process that caused your depression is being reversed. Satan's lies are now being replaced by God's truth.

2. IDENTIFY AND USE REALITY (GOD'S TRUTH)

The second thing God told me I must do to overcome my depression was to identify reality (God's Truth) and use it.

Before sharing with you the "how to" of this, let's review for a moment to set the stage. We have learned psychological depression is a matter of perspective (how we see things to be). Our negative perspective is caused by distorted thoughts resulting from faulty thinking. Thus, the solution is to change our thinking. How are we to do this? The answer God showed me is so simple it can be easily missed. We simply expose our thoughts to reality. This will reveal the distortion of our own thoughts. These spiritual exercises will enable us to change our thinking by replacing our distorted thoughts (Satan's lies) with reality.

What is reality? What is the truth? What is the real in this world? It is what God says. It is God's Word, the Bible. It is not what *I* think or say – that is only my view. It is not what *others* think or say – that is only their view. What God thinks and says is alone reality and truth. It is recorded for us in the Bible.

This is, of course, a doctrinal belief of the Christian faith. Does this mean that unless I am a Christian and hold to this faith about the Bible, this exercise will not help me overcome my depression? The answer is an emphatic no. A man from Florida with a doctorate from Oxford University was one of the most pathetic and hopeless depressives I have ever seen. He had been hospital-ized numerous times with several attempts at suicide. Just a week after being discharged from a hospital with the advice that they could do nothing to help him, he, by a strange course of events, ended up attending the seminar in which I share the information contained in this book. He was not a Christian and didn't even have a Bible. When he and his mother-in-law, who had told him about the seminar and attended with him, got to her home, he asked her for a Bible. Within an hour after the seminar, they sat together at her kitchen table with the Bible and his composition book and began to do these spiritual exercises. As he faithfully continued to do them, after several weeks he was able to return to Florida and to his top-level job which he had been unable to do for six months. He had a new life; he had gotten out of his pit of depression.

When this man's experience was related to me, I was as-tounded the exercises had accomplished so much for one who was not even a believer. Perhaps you may find this puzzling also.

During my striving to understand this, the Holy Spirit re-minded me of the biblical account of Jesus healing the man blind from birth. The Pharisees, already antagonized by the claims and actions of Jesus and ever wanting to impugn Him, repeatedly questioned the man about this Jesus. "I don't know whether He is good or bad," the man replied, "but I know this: *I was blind, and now I see!*" (John 9:25, TLB). Verses 35-38 clearly confirm the healed man knew nothing about the Messiah and was not a believer at the time he was healed. After his healing and his conversation with Jesus, he became a believer. Who wouldn't?

Wow! Hard to miss that truth. God was certainly teaching me something you and I both need to know: The Word of God (Bible) is so powerful, its power to heal is not limited by the spiritual status of the individual. When God so chooses, His Word com-bined with the work of His Holy Spirit can heal even the unbe-liever who is willing to approach Him with a sincere, humble, thirsting, and needy heart. Whoever you are and whatever your faith, I encourage you to do the exercises and leave the results to God.

THE SECOND SPIRITUAL EXERCISE

God revealed the step-by-step procedure of this exercise to enable me to carry out the second thing He told me I must do: identify and use reality (God's Truth):

1. Select a Book From the New Testament and Begin to Read It.

"Lord, I have read the Bible all my life. This is nothing new," I responded.

He quickly disclosed this was something new. Before I had read and studied it devotionally, to pass a college or seminar course, to teach a lesson, or prepare a sermon. What was new, was my *purpose* in reading it. Now I was to read it with only one purpose in mind — to identify and discover the truth about a believer. I was to focus only on two things: What the believer is and has in Christ. Note: In the Bible there are some promises made to a believer beyond basic salvation that are based on additional conditions. These are not to be considered for our purpose here. Focus only on what the believer is and has based solely on his acceptance of Jesus Christ as his personal Savior and Lord. This will insure that the truth (reality) we identify here applies to *every* believer.

Admittedly, in my depression I had not been particularly interested in reading my Bible, though previously I had taken great delight in doing so. Do not be surprised if you also feel this disinterest. It is common for depressed persons. However, when God focused me on the particular purpose contained in this exercise, and I saw it as a possible means to deliverance from my depression, my interest in reading the Bible was renewed.

I selected 1 Peter. Though you may choose any book in the New Testament, I would suggest you begin with 1 Peter also. Using The Living Bible, I expectantly began with the first verse of the first chapter. Immediately I began to see what God wanted me to discover. The second verse was full of truth about who I am and what I have as a believer. Hear this: "Dear friends, God the father chose you long ago and knew you would become His children. And the Holy Spirit has been at work in your hearts, cleansing you with the blood of Jesus Christ and making you to please Him. May God bless you richly and grant you increasing freedom from all anxiety and fear" (1 Peter 1:2, TLB).

I was amazed. Hadn't I ever read that verse before? Of course, I had, many times. But this was different. The Holy Spirit was revealing God's truth to speak to me at the point of my immediate pressing need: depression and all its oppressive feelings. God's eternal Word became God's current relevant Word. It had something wonderful to say to me exactly where I was – in the pit of depression.

2. Personalize the Scriptural Truths.

The next step was to personalize this. I was to put it into words that related it directly and personally to me. Doing this helps me to claim it as my own.

3. Write It in the Composition Book.

After personalizing the truths of the verse in my mind, God indicated I was to write it in my composition book. Turning to a page in my book, I wrote down these personalized truths from this same verse quoted above, 1 Peter 1:2, TLB.

...I *am* a child of God because God the Father chose me long ago.

...I *have* the Holy Spirit at work in my heart, cleansing me with the blood of Jesus and making me pleasing to Him.

...I *have* God to bless me and grant me increasing freedom from all anxiety and fear.

As I continued to read, truths seemed to leap off the pages. Thoughtfully I personalized them and added them to my composition book under "1 Peter." (See APPENDIX THREE.)

4. Read Aloud the Personalized Scriptural Truths You Have Written.

God taught me this step is vital. Without reading them aloud, the first three steps lose their full potential. I have already shared with you the importance of the words we speak. They shape, influence, and determine the quality of our life.

I had no problem accepting the importance of this step. I was very much aware of the disastrous effect of my negative statements. Since my words impact the quality of my life, I could use the principle to work for me instead of against me. Verbalizing positive truths would produce positive results.

Even though I accepted its importance, I found it difficult to read aloud these truths I had written. I really didn't understand why, and still don't. I can only assume it was related to my depression.

As I sat in my den with my Bible and notebook in my lap, I knew I needed help with this. I called Alma to sit beside me on the sofa. This was the first time I had shared with her my notebook and what God was having me do. I will never forget that morning. I asked her to read aloud with me these words I had written. My voice was faltering and broken with sobs. But the weeping was not all from sadness. There was a strange feeling of joy emerging. In my spirit I sensed new light that was going to guide me out of this depression. As the Spirit bore witness to her of my ray of hope, Alma began to weep wlth me as together we read over and over and over again, "I am a child of God...."

5. Spend Time Every Day Doing This Exercise.

Each day I was to devote time to this spiritual exercise. When I finished 1 Peter, I did 2 Peter, then other books of the New Testament and Psalms: identifying who I am and what I have as a believer in Christ, personalizing it, and adding it to the pages of my notebook. When I read aloud, I would read not only what I had written that day, but previous days also.

In doing this second exercise, I discovered specific verses that refuted my negative thoughts which I had written in my notebook in the first exercise, "Testing the Thought." I wrote the verses in the spaces I had left blank after each of my negative thoughts. In time, God refuted my every negative thought by His Word (reality).

— 15

Victory: Freedom at Last!

It did not occur overnight. Yet, as I faithfully and consistently did these spiritual exercises every day, a wonderful, and seemingly strange to some, phenomenon occurred.

Wonderful? Indeed so! It is one of the most wonderful experiences of my life, for it turned my life right side up. Over the next several months, as I spent time each day with my Bible and composition book doing the spiritual exercises, my thinking gradually but surely changed. With that change, my feelings and actions also changed. My depression symptoms increasingly diminished with each passing day until at last they were gone. I could think clearly, function, create, and enjoy life again.

By pure resolve and toughing out many sleepless nights, I hadn't taken a sleeping pill since I left the hospital. By now I had gradually taken myself off the antidepressant. (This should always be done gradually and with your physician's consent.) I had not seen my psychiatrist in two months, but I had another visit scheduled. I telephoned him, thanked him for his help, told him I was over my depression and didn't need him any longer, and canceled the appointment. Since 1986 I have not needed any of these again.

At last, I was free of my depression! The big black cloud had lifted. I was out of the miserable pit and back from the horrible world of the depressed. All of these terrible images and analogies of my depression that had flooded my mind, had now turned positive. The victory was mine. I was free at last.

There are no words to adequately convey to you the abounding joy and gratitude to God that filled my heart. My family knows because it filled their hearts also. Alma had her husband back. Kathy, Becky, Berny, and Randy had their dad back. My grandchildren had their granddaddy back. And I had my life back! The joy and gratitude continue to overflow. They always will. They are eternal.

It is, along with my deep compassion for depressed persons, the motivation for my focusing my ministry on helping others prevent and overcome depression. It is human to ask "why" when bad things happen to us. I often cried, "Why, God, why did You allow me to be so depressed?" This new focus God has given my ministry – in my depression I was convinced my ministry was only history – surely provides part of the answer. The apostle Paul explains: "What a wonderful God we have – He is the Father of our Lord Jesus Christ, the source of every mercy, and the one who so wonderfully comforts and strengthens us in our hardships and trials. And why does He do this? So that when others are troubled, needing our sympathy and encouragement, we can pass on to them this same help and comfort God has given us" (2 Corinthians 1:3-4, TLB).

Surely it is easy for all to agree, this was indeed a wonderful joyous experience for me and all who loved and had hurt with me. Yet, I am confident to some it will appear strange that it was the spiritual therapy, these simple spiritual exercises, that enabled me to overcome my depression.

The simplicity of God's ways often *appears* strange. This should not surprise us because the Bible warns: "God has deliberately chosen to use ideas the world considers foolish and of little worth in order to shame those people considered by the world as wise and great" (1 Corinthians 1:27, TLB).

Spiritual therapy will appear strange and even perhaps doubtful only to those who seek to understand it with their intellect. By human means, it is beyond understanding. Spiritual wonders can only be spiritually understood. The Bible declares, "The natural man receiveth not the things of the Spirit of God; for they are foolishness unto him; neither can he know them, because they are spiritually discerned" (1 Corinthians 2:14, KJV).

Therefore, how the spiritual exercises can effectively prevent and overcome depression, must first be understood spiritually. Only then will it appear logical and practical.

How are we to understand it spiritually? God explains: When we "welcome the Word" it is "implanted and rooted [in your heart]" and "contains power to save your souls" (James 1:21, AMP). As you read and speak His Word, the Holy Spirit implants and roots it in your heart (mind). It becomes a part of your innermost being. It exposes and rids you of Satan's lies, and replaces them with God's truth.

What happens here is the fulfillment of the claim the Bible makes for itself: "The whole Bible (literally, every Scripture) was given to us by inspiration from God and is useful *to teach us what is true,* and *to make us realize what is wrong in our lives;* [and] *it straightens us out* and *helps us do what is right"* (2 Timothy 3:15, TLB).

The result? As quoted above, the Bible says this "saves your souls." What does "saves" mean? In the New Testament's original language (Greek), it means all of these things: to restore, to heal, to save from disease and its effects, to deliver from sin and its consequences, and to preserve from danger. It is a marvelous word describing an amazing experience. What is your soul? Your soul is your mind, emotions, and will. Thus, it heals and restores your thinking, feelings, and actions. *It changes your thinking! It slays the giant depression!*

Even after you have overcome your depression, it is important to continue the spiritual exercises daily in order to stay free. I must confess that now I allow busy days to slip by without doing them in spite of knowing better. But if I sense negative thoughts beginning to invade my mind and begin to have depressive feelings, I immediately grab my composition book and daily do the spiritual exercises, especially reading aloud God's truth (reality) as to who I am and what I possess in Christ.

As we maintain the exercises, God continues to root and embed His truth in our innermost being. This enables us to immediately identify and reject Satan's lies as he injects them into our thoughts or through the words of others. It prevents us from ever again accepting Satan's lies as reality and being overcome with depression. Just as the Alcoholics Anonymous member can never lay aside The Twelve Steps and remain sober, neither can the depressive ever lay aside his Bible and depression notebook and remain free of depression. They must be our companions for the remainder of our life. If they gather dust, our minds become vulnerable to faulty thinking. If faulty thinking occurs, depression will follow.

Though depression is considered by most secular therapists to be recurring, it doesn't have to be. Spiritual therapy not only enables the depressed person overcome depression, but also stay free of it.

My lips shall forever echo these words of the Apostle Paul, "Thanks be unto God, who giveth us the victory through our Lord Jesus Christ" (1 Corinthians 15:57, KJV).

At last the victory over depression was mine! To God be all the glory!

— 16 ————————————

How to Help a Depressed Person

Depressed persons hurt. So do all who love and care about them. Depression is almost as painful for family members and close friends as it is for the depressed person.

I can vividly remember my feelings of frustration, helplessness, and fear as I saw my dad slip deeper and deeper into the pit of depression. I was a freshman in college (which means it has been a long time ago), but in my memory I can still feel his pain, my mother's, my brother's, and mine.

As a pastor I also experienced this frustration when depressed parishioners and their families sought my help. Even with my training in psychology and psychiatry, my desire to help far exceeded my ability to do so. (This was prior to my own depression and God revealing to me the principles and spiritual exercises I have shared in this book.)

Listen to the hurt and frustration of this participant in my seminar in Norwich, England, who wrote to me, "One of my closest friends, whom I love as dearly as my own family, has been suffering from clinical depression for over three years. She appears such a hopeless case. She feels herself to have been universally rejected and abandoned by the medical profession, by her friends and by God. As her dear friend, I have what seems to me to be an insurmountable problem. How can I, a person whom she no longer trusts, bring her a message from a God in whom she no longer believes?"

This letter is not unusual. I receive many similar letters and telephone calls. Basically the cry is always the same: "I am so frustrated. How can I help my loved one who is so depressed?"

If you have ever had someone you love overcome by depression, you can identify with these feelings. You care deeply and earnestly desire to help, but feel so helpless. Your pain in witnessing their pain is almost unbearable. You become anxious for your loved one. How much worse is the depression going to get? Will he survive this horrible experience? Where will it end? Will this one you love and care for so dearly ever again be free to be the person he really is? Your frustration mounts. You want so badly to help, but don't know what or how.

Eventually you may have to battle your impatience. Depressed persons can become quite exasperating. You may feel like giving up on them even though having such a thought makes you feel guilty.

Depression is a very painful experience, not only for the depressed person, but for all who share life with him in a significant way. All family members and friends who want and try to help will experience these feelings of pain, frustration, and impatience. Don't be surprised or overcome by them.

Most everyone who seeks to help a depressed person begins from a point of great disadvantage. Why? Because it is impossible to completely understand what depression is really like, unless you have been depressed yourself. There is no doubt in my mind that this is true. At one point in my life, I was convinced that because of my training I understood depression. Yet when I experienced clinical depression myself, I discovered I really knew or understood very little about it. The major and most important portion of what I now know, comes from my own experience of being depressed, and what in that experience God revealed to me. What I learned in my earlier training has become clearer and more understandable to me in retrospect because of my own depression.

But hear this! This does not mean that unless you have been depressed yourself, you can't help a person who is. You can help a depressed person without experiencing it yourself. The more you know and understand about depression, however, the more you are able to help. And, it is definitely possible for you to know more.

I have been privileged to visit the Holy Land six times. What an experience that is for a Christian. It is more than a trip, it is also a spiritual high. Now you can't completely and fully know what it is like unless you visit the Holy Land. But, if you see my slides and hear my experiences and feelings from my visits, you will definitely know more than you did before.

The same applies to depression. Having read this book, you have vicariously shared my knowledge and experience of depression. You have felt my pain, shared my feelings, tasted my despair, and learned what God shared with me. For sure, you know and understand depression more than before. Now you can better comprehend what your depressed person experiences, feels, thinks, and fears. Because you do, you can be to him one who understands. You *can* be his helper!

SUGGESTED WAYS TO HELP

Generally, you can help a depressed person by sharing information from this book. Most persons in the midst of their depression actually know very little about it. They may not even recognize their problem is depression, even though they are well aware something is terribly wrong. They know the thoughts and feelings they are experiencing, but do not recognize these to be the classic symptoms of depression. You can now help him recognize this. Simply to know there is someone (you) who does understand his thoughts, feelings, and fears is very encouraging and helpful. You can help him understand the kinds and levels, to come to grips with the real cause, and inform him of the various kinds of therapy. Most importantly, inform and encourage him to apply the spiritual therapy (Bible verses, principles, and exercises) to his own depression.

Now, in addition, let me suggest some specific do's and do not's for helping a depressed person.

THINGS TO DO

1. Do Spend Time With Him.

Be with him as much as reasonable and possible. Your presence says a great deal and provides much help and support. Don't avoid being with a depressed person because you don't know what to say. Do not think you have to always be saying something. Be a good listener. In the beginning let your presence do most of your talking.

2. Do Be Very Patient.

It is tempting to get discouraged and give up on a depressed person. He holds on so tenaciously to his negative thoughts and feelings which you recognize to be so very distorted. Remember from his perspective they are reality. Anyone who insists on continuing to wallow in self-pity can become very grating to others. Be patient. Don't give up. Having someone you love give up on you is a damaging blow to one already depressed. But having someone refuse to give up on you, even when you have given up on yourself, is extremely supportive.

How eternally grateful I am that even during the depth of my depression, my wife, children, and some special friends never gave up on me. I could not have blamed them if they had. The fact they didn't, played a larger role in my recovery than they will ever know. But I know. Their love, patience, and perseverance were some of the early rungs on the ladder by which I was eventually able to climb out of the pit of depression.

3. Do Give Understanding and Empathy.

The depressed person feels very isolated, all alone in a strange world. Even though he knows others care, he feels they just don't understand what he is thinking and feeling. He desperately longs for someone who understands. If you have experienced and overcome depression, or even if you haven't, but have become informed about depression, you can be that someone. Focus your relationship with him on being that someone. You may say, "I hear you telling me you feel depressed (or whatever feeling they have just shared with you)." Don't say, "I understand *why* you feel...." This tends to justify his depressed feelings.

4. Do Endeavor to Instill and Program Hope.

To the depressed person: his goals have been destroyed, his outlook is all negative, and he envisions no solution to his problems. His thought patterns are focused on failure and hopelessness, causing circumstances to appear many times blacker than they really are. Bring some "light" to his thinking. Endeavor to instill hope. Share the stories of your and others victories over bad circumstances and depressed feelings.

Here is another important way to instill hope. Get him to say out loud with you, "I can overcome depression!" Print these words on some post-it notes. With his assistance, place them in prominent places where he will be forced to see them many times during the day: bathroom mirror, refrigerator, desk, doors, television, dashboard of car, etc. Ask him, as a favor to you, to read it out loud every time he sees it. If he is reluctant or indicates he really can't believe these words, assure him that for now that is all right. Insist, to the degree that you can, that he say it anyway. He doesn't realize it now, but this is verbalizing a positive statement and in time will change his thinking. You will discover other ways to be an encourager and instill hope.

5. Do Suggest Thoughts to Help Change His Perspective.

Always be alert to opportunities to suggest thoughts that may help change his perspective. This can be a planted "seed" that yields much fruit.

A wise friend said to me when in my depression I was convinced we would never sell my deceased grandfather's house, "French, have you considered that somewhere there is a young couple who would love to have that house and restore it. Soon they may come along and buy it." No, I had not considered that possibility. It was far too positive a thought for me to have. But her saying it injected that possibility into my thinking. Note she did not argue against my view, she just asked me if I had considered another possibility.

6. Do Try to Get Him to Feel Better About Himself.

The depressed person's self-image has been shredded. It is predominantly self-inflicted, but, of course, can be aided by critical comments and actions of others. Your goal is to make him feel better about himself. His self-image is often so annihilated, compliments are impossible for him to believe. If you will remind him of some specific accomplishments from his past, however, it will cast doubt on his conviction that he is a total failure. While I was battling my depression, occasionally someone would say or write to me: "Often I read my notes from the teachings you shared years ago, and they are still such a tremendous help to me"; or "I will never forget how much you meant to our family when my father died." These came as refreshing drops of rain to parched ground. You can provide raindrops for a depressed person's desert.

7. Do Try to Get Him to Think About Something Besides Himself.

The boundaries of the depressed person's world are very narrow, extending very little beyond self. When he talks, it centers on himself. This is the way he is and where he is coming from just now.

It is a hard door to drive a wedge in, but you can help. Share news of some current events or experiences with him. Be sure they are not negative. The last thing he needs is to hear about your cousin being raped, the government raising taxes, or the increase in violent crime. Share good news about people you both know. Bring up subjects that previously were of special interest to him such as sports, movies, cooking, etc. Keep priming the pump and eventually he will begin to converse with you about these things.

8. Do Get Him to Engage in Activities.

Most depressed persons are withdrawn and their energy gauge reads zero. Even if they know it would help them to do something, they usually don't feel able to. Encourage your depressed person to do something with you. He will probably be reluctant, maybe even resistant. Be prepared for this. Meet his resistance with your insistence. This is one occasion when it is all right to be pushy. Your efforts will reap double benefits if you get him to do something he used to do but thinks he can't do anymore. This will help with his self-image by refuting his conviction he can't do it now. For example, helping you with a project, fishing, or a game of golf. If your depressed person is a woman who has always baked cakes, but now declares she can't, try this. Go to the store, buy all the ingredients, bring them to her house, and say, "Let's get in your kitchen. I want you to show me how to make one of those delicious cakes you make!" It may appear to you as a trivial activity, but to the depressed person it will be a big accomplishment. And great wars are won by a succession of small victories.

9. Do Share Anything That You Have Experienced or Learned That Has Been Helpful in Dealing With Negative Depressed Feelings.

It is not wise to immediately start giving counsel or advice. By your caring, listening, understanding, and patience build a bond with your depressed person. Even though he may be a family member or a close friend of long standing, this still needs to be done. In many respects he is a different person with an altogether different perspective from the person you have known. Upon recovery he will be that person again, but now he is in another world, the world of the depressed, and you need to bond with him as the depressed person he now is. You need to discover who he is now, and where he is coming from. As the bond strengthens and he begins to trust you and sense in you one who understands, then you can begin to share and help him understand depression and how to overcome it. What God shared with me about depression and how to overcome it, He has shared with you through me. I have no doubt He will use you to share it with a depressed person so he too may experience freedom. Make it yours, then share it.

10. Do Seek to Remove All Weapons, Poisonous Substances, Medications, Etc., From Accessibility.

Never assume your depressed person is not suicidal just because he never speaks of it. Many will have suicidal thoughts, but few will make them known. Do not take the risk. In as far as possible, remove any possible means he could use to take his own life. Short of locking a person in a suicidal-proof room, you can't totally remove the possibility of suicide. But removing as many means as possible will make it more difficult for him. The difficulty and the additional time and effort required by it may be just enough to cause him to rethink his intentions.

11. Do Take Him for Professional Help If the Depression Becomes Severe.

Depression is not just a miserable state; it can become a life or death matter. When the person becomes severely depressed, he needs professional help. It is much easier on everyone concerned if your depressed person agrees. Even if he resists, you must get him there even if you have to resort to legal means. Remember the depressed person's ability to think and make decisions is greatly impaired. He needs you to make the right decision for him while he is unable to do so for himself. This responsibility rightfully belongs to the family of the depressed person. But if for any reason they will not or cannot do so, a close friend needs to assume it. Real love requires us at times to do some tough things. It requires us to do what a loved one *needs* us to do, not what he *wants* us to do.

CAUTION: THINGS NOT TO DO

1. Do Not Help Him Justify His Self-Pity or Depression.
He must stop justifying his depression in order to overcome it. Therefore, be sure you don't, by your actions or words, help him hold on to his justification. Never say, "Wow, no wonder you are depressed. You certainly have every right to be. Anybody would who has been through what you have." It may give him a brief sense of relief, but actually it is very damaging. It enforces his "victim" complex.

2. Do Not Condemn or Make Him Feel Guilty for Being Depressed.
Being depressed is hideous enough. Feeling guilty for being depressed adds to the misery. So never say or do anything to make him feel condemned or guilty. Caution, never say, "You don't have any reason to be depressed. It is silly for you to feel sorry for yourself." To the depressed person this will be interpreted as rejection though you don't intend it to be. It will cause him to feel you don't understand, and greatly impair your role as helper.

3. Do Not Be Overly Cheerful.
To help a depressed person many people believe they must

overflow with cheerfulness when they visit. Their objective is to "cheer up" this sad person. It is a noble goal, but caution must be exercised. Overly exuberant cheerfulness in one seeking to help, can be hurtful to a person struggling to stay alive in the pit of depression. It does not cheer up the depressed person. The obvious contrast only makes him sadder. It makes it almost impossible for him to identify with you, interfering with and not strengthening your bond. The Bible warns, "Being happy-go-lucky around a person whose heart is heavy is as bad as stealing his jacket in cold weather or rubbing salt in his wounds" (Proverbs 25:20, TLB). When visiting your depressed person, be as natural as you can. Avoid extremes of cheerfulness or sadness. A warm smile that says I love and care about you accomplishes far more than boisterous laughter.

4. Do Not Argue.

Be careful not to argue with a depressed person. Most all of his expressed thoughts and opinions will seem distorted and even ridiculous to you. But he is so convinced they are real, your arguing a point with him will harm and not help. It will cause him to defend his views, thus entrenching them more deeply in his mind. Your arguing will be perceived by him as your inability to understand and rejection, and thus harm your relationship. Instead of arguing, seek to inject an alternate thought by saying, "Have you considered this possibility?..."

5. Do Not Play the Role of His Professional Therapist.

A helping family member or friend should never play the role of amateur psychiatrist or psychologist. Even the most avid viewer of television soaps and talk shows or reader of popular magazines is not qualified for this role. Do not make suggestions with regard to the use of any particular antidepressant medication regardless of what your experience has been with one. Do not delve into his past seeking to uncover some deep dark reason for his troubled condition. If this is needed, it is the job of highly trained professionals. Even they proceed with great caution. At the medical school psychiatric staff conferences I attended, the department head was always cautioning the interns and residents, "Be sure you don't dig up anything you are not capable of covering up." That is excellent advice for anyone seeking to help any troubled person.

6. Do Not Underestimate Your Importance as a Helper.

Emphatically do not underestimate your potential as a helper. If the depression is not too intense an understanding, caring, patient family member or close friend may be all a depressed person needs to help him overcome his depression. Even in severe cases where a professional therapist and possibly hospitalization is needed, your continued relationship will be the cornerstone of his support and encouragement. Do not lessen or withdraw your help and support even though others become involved. Recognize their role, but recognize yours as well. You are an anchor your depressed person can't dare lose.

7. Do Not Assume the Responsibility for His Recovery.

Recognize the importance of your role as a helper, but never assume the responsibility to get your depressed person over his depression. As we stated previously, if he is severely clinically depressed, there are some actions you may have to take for him. Even then, the responsibility to get him well is not yours. Ultimately, every depressed person has to assume the responsibility for his own recovery. You can't do it for him, therefore don't assume to. I am convinced depressed persons can overcome their depression. Yet the fact is some don't. Do not load yourself up with a bundle of guilt if yours doesn't. It isn't your fault. Years ago, as a young pastor, I read somewhere (the source I have long forgotten, but the message I never will) that there were some persons that even Jesus couldn't help because they wouldn't receive it. Time and time again, the Holy Spirit has brought that truth to my mind as I wept over the hurt and pain of a person I had been unable to help. All of us who care and seek to help need to remember — we are neither God nor the troubled person, only their helper. You must not attempt to do what only they can do, simply be willing to do what you can do. Then leave the outcome to God and your depressed person. You can do no more.

CONCLUSION

Your reading this chapter means that you care about those who suffer the living hell of depression. I thank you for caring, and pray I have encouraged you in your desire and ability to help. Do not be discouraged by the number of suggestions I have made. Few, if any of us, can excel at doing all of them. But that isn't as important as your willingness to be used.

The persons who helped me the most did not know everything about depression or how to help me. But they loved me when I didn't love myself, and believed in me when I had lost faith in myself. They kept telling me that until I could begin to believe it for myself.

I am pleased by your desire to learn all you can about helping a depressed person. The more you know, the better prepared you are to help. But whatever you know, combined with your love, understanding, and patience, will enable God to use you to help a depressed person.

The Last Word

Will this spiritual therapy get me or my loved one out of depression? I hope you are now asking this question. After all, that is the "bottom line."

I believe with all of my being that spiritual therapy is the only way to really "fix" psychological depression — to get completely and lastingly over it. Yet I would be totally dishonest and irresponsible if I answered that absolutely and positively it will get *you* or your loved one over depression. As much as I would like to, I cannot assure you of that because I do not know.

Let me tell you what I do know. I know accepting the principles and doing the exercises God shared with me, and I have shared with you, got me completely over my depression when the secular therapy had not. Since 1986 I have been free of abnormal depression using only spiritual therapy.

I do know others have shared they also have been set free by using this spiritual therapy. Let me encourage you by sharing the stories of just two of them:

It worked for the young lady bank teller in South Carolina. After participating in the seminar and putting it into practice, she wrote to me: "During my childhood and since, I haven't known a single day without depression. Thanks to the Lord and your seminar, for the very first time in my life, I am free of depression. I would not dare let a single day pass without doing my spiritual exercises."

I do know what happened in the life of a man in Michigan. This is a portion of his letter to me: "I'm a forty-one-year-old man and have lived with a severe depression most of my adult life. My illness was misdiagnosed many times, *many times* over the years. It was finally recognized in 1988. I have spent a total of eight months in the hospital over the last four years on four separate visits. I have attempted suicide twice and came very close. I have read many books and tapes and have never found any answers. I have never felt so hopeless. The depression was bad enough it left me unable to work. People who have never experienced severe depression can't imagine the fear, anxiety, and feelings of hopelessness. I received the tapes of your seminar two months ago from a loving, caring uncle who lives in Florida. God through you and your tapes has turned my world right side up. Listening to your tapes brought tears to my eyes. We have so much in common. It was so inspiring to listen to a man who has walked in my shoes and licked it. I am now happily self-employed and *enjoy* a totally different outlook on life in general. As an ultra-perfectionist, I needed to change my character and my thinking. Please excuse all my mistakes in this handwritten letter, but it is the first letter I have written in four years."

As I read this letter, I was crying so loudly Alma rushed from another room to see what was wrong with me. To ease her alarm, I quickly assured her they were tears of joy. I felt this man's pain and hurt, but how I rejoiced that God had given him the victory. I gave Alma the letter to read. Then we both wept from sheer joy.

Every time I read this letter I marvel that in this man's experience are many of the ingredients we have talked about. You probably recognize them, but let me highlight some: a depressed person; a loving caring person (his uncle) who shared with him (through the tapes) these truths about depression and these principles and exercises of spiritual therapy; his discovery there was someone (my experience shared on the tapes) who had walked where he was and understood what he was feeling; the hope instilled in him upon learning of my victory; his faithful practice of the spiritual therapy resulting in a change in his thinking and his character; and his experience of freedom from depression.

This is vital for you to know: Though I pray you find this book helpful, simply reading it will not get you or anyone out of depression. If you learn everything I have shared, it alone will not set you free. The principles must be *accepted* and the spiritual exercises *practiced,* if you are to overcome depression. Hearing it is not enough, spiritual therapy *must be done* to heal. Will spiritual therapy work for you? You alone may hold the answer to that question.

Let me encourage you to give God's spiritual therapy an opportunity to heal you. If it set me and others free, there is every expectation that practicing it will work for you. We were no different than you are...hurting persons desperately wanting to have our life back.

I have always treasured these words of the psalmist: "I bless the holy name of God with all my heart. Yes, I will bless the Lord and not forget the glorious things he does for me. He forgives all my sins. He heals me. He ransoms me with loving-kindness and tender mercies. He fills my life with good things! My youth is renewed like the eagle's!" (Psalm 103:1-5, TLB). After my depression and God getting me out of it, these words became even more meaningful. When I discovered the Amplified Bible translates verse 4: "Who redeems your life from the pit," I gratefully knew these words are indeed the story of my life.

Yes, I do bless the Lord with all my being for He has redeemed my life from the pit, the pit of depression. I firmly believe He wants to redeem you from your pit.

The words of an old gospel hymn, "Look Where He Brought Me From," express what is in my heart:

"He brought me out of the darkness into the morning light. Look where He brought me from. And I am more fascinated with the light, than the dark."

Come, my dear friend. Come join me in the light...it is far more fascinating than the darkness!

—— **Appendix One** ————————————————

Armory of Bible Verses

The Bible is the sword of the believer, its verses our spiritual weapons.

KEY VERSE:

My son, pay attention to what I say; listen to my words. Never let them get away from you. Remember them and keep them in your heart. They will give life and health to anyone who understands them. Be careful how you think; your life is shaped by your thoughts. Never say anything that isn't true. Have nothing to do with lies and misleading words (Proverbs 4:20-24, TEV).

PERSPECTIVE (The way you see and consider things to be):

Now your attitudes and thoughts must be constantly changing for the better (Ephesians 4:23, TLB).

Your attitude should be the kind that was shown us by Jesus Christ (Philippians 2:5, TLB).

For it may be that God will give them the opportunity to repent and come to know the truth. And then they will come to their senses and escape from the trap of the devil, who caught them and made them obey his will (2 Timothy 2:25-26, TEV).

You must keep on believing the things you have been taught....You know how, when you were a small child, you were taught the Holy Scriptures (2 Timothy 3:14-15, TLB).

116

TRUTH (What God says. This alone is reality):

The whole Bible (literally, every Scripture) was given to us by inspiration from God and is useful to teach us what is true and to make us realize what is wrong in our lives; it straightens us out and helps us do what is right (2 Timothy 3:16, TLB).

With all these things in mind, dear brothers, stand firm and keep a strong grip on the truth that we taught you in our letters and during the time we were with you (2 Thessalonians 2:15, TLB).

Hold tight to the pattern of truth I taught you, especially concerning the faith and love Christ Jesus offers you (2 Timothy 1:13, TLB).

God's truth stands firm like a great rock and nothing can shake it (2 Timothy 2:19, TLB).

For there is going to come a time when people won't listen to the truth, but will go around looking for teachers who will tell them just what they want to hear. They won't listen to what the Bible says, but will blithely follow their own misguided ideas (2 Timothy 4:3-4, TLB).

I have been sent to bring faith to those God has chosen and to teach them to know God's truth – the kind of truth that changes lives – so that they can have eternal life (Titus 1:12, TLB).

And now just as you trusted Christ to save you, trust Him too for each day's problems, live in vital union with Him. Let your roots grow down into Him and draw up nourishment from Him. See that you go on growing in the Lord and become strong and vigorous in the truth you were taught. Let your lives overflow with joy and thanksgiving for all He has done. Don't let others spoil your faith and joy with their philosophies, their wrong shallow answers built on men's thoughts and ideas, instead of on what Christ has done. For in Christ there is all of God in a human body; so you have everything when you have Christ, and you are filled with God through your union with Christ. He is the highest ruler and authority over every other power (Colossians 2:6-10, TLB).

You came up out of death with Him into a new life because you trusted the Word of the Mighty God who raised Christ from the dead (Colossians 2:12, TLB).

Remember what Christ taught and let His words enrich your lives and make you wise (Colossians 3:16, TLB).

Then we will no longer be like children, forever changing our minds about what we believe because someone has told us something different, or has cleverly lied to us and made the lie sound like the truth. Instead, we will lovingly follow the truth at all times – speaking truly, dealing truly, living truly – and so become more and more in every way like Christ, who is the Head of His Body, the Church (Ephesians 4:14-15, TLB).

Let me say this then, speaking for the Lord. Live no longer as the unsaved do, for they are blinded and confused. Their closed hearts are full of darkness, they are far away from the life of God because they have shut their minds against Him, and they cannot understand His ways (Ephesians 4:17-18, TLB).

THOUGHTS OR THINKING (The opinion, idea, or perception that dwells in your mind and thus determines your feelings and actions):

Keep a close watch on all you do or think. Stay true to what is right and God will bless you and use you to help others (2 Timothy 4:16, TLB).

Let heaven fill your thoughts, and don't spend your time worrying about things down here (Colossians 3:2, TLB).

Now your thoughts and attitudes must all be constantly changing for the better (Ephesians 4:23, TLB).

Fix your thoughts on what is true and good and right. Think about things that are pure and lovely, and dwell on the fine good things in others. Think about all you can praise God for and be glad about it (Philippians 4:8, TLB).

It is true that we live in the world, but we do not fight from worldly motives. The weapons we use in our fight are not the world's weapons, but God's powerful weapons, which we use to destroy stongholds. We destroy false arguments; we pull down every proud obstacle that is raised against the knowledge of God; we take every thought captive and make it obey Christ (2 Corinthians 10:3-5, TEV).

What he (a man) thinks is what he really is (Proverbs 23:7, TEV).

SAY OR SPEAK (Words spoken from your mouth and lips):

May our Lord Jesus Christ Himself and God our Father, who has loved us and given us everlasting comfort and hope which we don't deserve, comfort your hearts with all comfort and help you in every good thing you say and do (2 Thessalonians 2:16-17, TLB).

If you want a happy good life, keep control of your tongue and guard your lips from telling lies (1 Peter 3:10, TLB).

A man's moral self shall be filled with the fruit of his mouth, and with the consequence of his words he must be satisfied (whether good or evil). Death and life are in the power of the tongue, and they who indulge it shall eat the fruit of it (for death or life) (Proverbs 18:20-21, AMP).

Don't you understand? Anything that goes into a person's mouth goes into his stomach and then out of his body. But the things that come out of the mouth come from the heart, and these are the things that make a person ritually unclean. For from his heart come the evil ideas which lead him to kill, commit adultery, and do other immoral things, to rob, lie, and slander others. These are the things that make a person unclean (Matthew 15:17-20, TEV).

SPIRITUAL EXERCISES (Time and energy spent in improving our total well-being by focusing on what pertains to our spiritual well-being):

Spend your time and energy in the exercise of keeping spiritually fit. Bodily exercise is all right, but spiritual exercise is much more important and is a tonic for all you do. So exercise yourself spiritually and practice being a better Christian, because that will help you not only now in this life, but in the next one too (1 Timothy 4:7-8, TLB).

Know what His Word says and means (2 Timothy 2:15, TLB).

And now just as you trusted Christ to save you, trust Him too for each day's problems; live in vital union with Him (Colossians 2:6, TLB).

Do you want more and more of God's kindness and peace? Then learn to know Him better and better (2 Peter 1:2, TLB).

Oh, the joys of those who do not follow evil men's advice, who do not hang around with sinners, scoffing at the things of God; But they delight in doing everything God wants them to, and day and night are always meditating on His laws and thinking about ways to follow Him more closely (Psalm 1:1-2, TLB).

Testing the Thought

(An Example of the First Spiritual Exercise in Chapter 14)

KEY VERSE (Taking every thought captive):

The weapons we use in our fight are not the world's weapons but God's powerful weapons, which we use to destroy strongholds. We destroy false arguments; we pull down every proud obstacle that is raised against the knowledge of God; *we take every thought captive* and make it obey Christ (2 Corinthians 10:4-5, TEV).

1. MY THOUGHT: GOD DOES NOT LOVE ME ANYMORE!

REALITY (GOD'S TRUTH): The Father Himself loves you dearly because you love me and believe that I (Jesus) came from the Father (John 16:27, TLB).

And may you be able to feel and understand, as all God's children should, how long, how wide, how deep, and how high His love really is; and to experience this love for yourselves, though it is so great that you will never see the end of it or fully know or understand it. And so at last you will be filled up with God Himself (Ephesians 3:18-19, TLB).

2. MY THOUGHT: GOD HAS WITHDRAWN HIMSELF FROM ME. I FEEL FORSAKEN BY GOD!

REALITY (GOD'S TRUTH): For God has said, "I will never, never fail you nor forsake you" (Hebrews 13:5b, TLB).

3. MY THOUGHT: MY SINS ARE SO BAD AND SO MANY THAT GOD COULD NEVER FORGIVE ME!

REALITY (GOD'S TRUTH): Christ forgave all my sins, and blotted out the charges proved against me, the list of His commands which I had not obeyed (Colossians 2:13b-14, TLB).

4. I HAVE COME TO GOD SO MANY TIMES FOR HIS HELP AND FORGIVENESS, THEN FAILED HIM AGAIN, THAT GOD JUST DOESN'T WANT ME AROUND ANY LONGER!

Now we can come fearlessly right into God's presence, assured of His glad welcome when I come with Christ and trust in Him (Ephesians 3:12, TLB).

5. I CAN'T DO ANYTHING RIGHT ANYMORE!

Christ has given each of us special abilities – whatever He wants us to have out of His rich storehouse of gifts (Ephesians 4:7, TLB).
Guard well the splendid God-given ability you received as a gift from the Holy Spirit who lives within you (2 Timothy 1:14, TLB).

6. I HAVE HAD IT. I DON'T HAVE ANY STRENGTH OR RESOURCES LEFT!

God will give His people strength, He will bless them with peace (Psalm 29:11, TLB).
Out of God's glorious unlimited resources, He will give you the mighty inner strengthening of His Holy Spirit (Ephesians 3:16, TLB).

7. THE FUTURE HOLDS NOTHING FOR ME!

I am truly glad for there is wonderful joy ahead for me even though the going is rough for a while down here (1 Peter 1:6, TLB).

We have been called to a glorious future (Ephesians 4:4b, TLB).

Yet what we suffer now is nothing compared to the glory He will give us later (Romans 8:18, TLB).

8. NO ONE CAN HELP ME. I AM NOT EVEN SURE GOD CAN!

God by His mighty power at work within us is able to do far more than we would ever dare to ask or even dream of — infinitely beyond our highest prayers, desires, thoughts, or hopes (Ephesians 3:20, TLB).

9. I AM SO UNWORTHY, TOO UNWORTHY TO EVEN COME TO GOD AND ASK HIM FOR HELP!

It was through what His Son did that God cleared a path for everything to come to Him...for Christ's death on the cross has made peace with God for all by His blood. This includes you who were so far away from God....He has brought you back as His friends. He has done this through the death on the cross of His own body, and now as a result Christ has brought you into the very presence of God, and you are standing there before Him with nothing left against you....The only condition is that you fully believe the Truth, standing in it steadfast and firm, strong in the Lord, convinced of the Good News that Jesus died for you, and never shifting from trusting Him to save you (Colossians 1:20-23b, TLB).

10. MY FAITH IN MYSELF HAS BEEN SHATTERED. I FEEL LIKE GOD DOESN'T BELIEVE IN ME ANYMORE!

Even when we are too weak to have any faith left, He remains faithful to us and will help us, for He cannot disown us who are part of Himself, and He will always carry out His promises to us (2 Timothy 2:13, TLB).

11. THERE ARE SO MANY EXPERIENCES AHEAD OF ME THAT I KNOW I WON'T BE ABLE TO HANDLE: THE POSSIBLE DEATH OF MY MATE, DETERIORATING HEALTH, MY OWN DEATH, ETC. I MIGHT AS WELL JUST GIVE UP NOW!

God is my shield, protecting me and guarding my pathway (Proverbs 2:8, TLB).

You (God) are my hiding place from every storm of life....You surround me with songs of victory (Psalm 32:7, TLB).

For I can do everything God asks me to do with the help of Christ who gives me the strength and power (Philippians 4:13, TLB).

12. I AM IN SUCH INNER TURMOIL. NEVER AGAIN WILL I KNOW THE PEACE OF MIND I ONCE KNEW!

I (Jesus) am leaving you with a gift – peace of mind and heart! And the peace I give you isn't fragile like the peace the world gives. So don't be troubled or afraid (John 14:27, TLB).

13. NOTHING EVER TURNS OUT GOOD FOR ME!

And we know that all that happens to us is working for our good if we love God and are fitting into His plans (Romans 8:28, TLB).

14. I AM A TOTAL FAILURE AT EVERYTHING!

I am a child of God because God the Father chose me long ago (1 Peter 1:2, TLB).

Yes, everything else is worthless when compared with the priceless gain of knowing Christ Jesus my Lord. I have put aside all else, counting it worth less than nothing, in order that I can have Christ, and become one with Him, no longer counting on being saved by being good enough or by obeying God's laws, but trusting Christ to save me; for God's way of making us right with Himself depends on faith – counting on Christ alone (Philippians 3:8-9, TLB).

Declaration of God's Truth

(An example of the Second Spiritual Exercise in Chapter 14)

A personalization of selected verses from 1 Peter, The Living Bible, to declare the reality of who I am and what I have as a believer in Christ Jesus. This is the real me.

I am a child of God because God the Father chose me long ago (1:2).

I have the Holy Spirit at work in my heart, cleansing me with the blood of Jesus and making me pleasing to Him (1:2).

I can expect God to bless me and grant me increasing freedom from all anxiety and fear (l:2).

I am born again because of the boundless mercy of God (1:3).

I am now a member of God's own family (1:3).

I live in the hope of eternal life because Christ rose again from the dead (l:3).

I have the gift of eternal life, and it is kept in heaven for me by God, pure and undefiled, beyond the reach of change and decay (1:4).

I will get there safely to receive it, because God in His mighty power will make sure of this and because I am trusting Him (1:5).

I am truly glad for there is wonderful joy ahead for me even though the going is rough for a while down here (1:6).

I am happy with the inexpressible joy that comes from heaven itself because I love Him and trust Him even though I have never seen Him (1:8).

I am saved (my sins are forgiven and forgotten by God) for

God paid for me with the precious blood of Christ, the sinless, spotless Lamb of God (1:19).

I can put my trust in God, the God who raised Christ from the dead. My faith and hope rests in Christ alone (1:21).

I can have real love for everyone because my soul has been cleansed from selfishness and hatred when I trusted Christ to save me (1:22).

I have a new life and it will last forever because it comes from Christ (1:23).

I am free to do God's will at all times (2:16).

I do not have to get even when I am attacked or insulted by others. I can leave my case in the hands of God who always judges fairly (2:23).

Jesus carried my sins in His own body when He died on the cross so that I can be finished with sin and live a good life from now on (2:24).

I am healed by Jesus' stripes (2:24).

Jesus is the guardian of my soul and I am kept safe from all attacks (2.25).

I do not have to be bewildered when I go through fiery trials for this is no strange or unusual thing and as I share Christ's sufferings I will afterwards have the wonderful joy of sharing Christ's glory (4:12-13).

I can be happy when I am cursed and insulted for being a Christian, for when that happens the Spirit of God will come upon me with great glory (4:14).

I can entrust myself to God for God has promised He will never fail me (4:19).

I can give God all my cares and worries for He is always thinking about me and watching everything that concerns me (5:7).

I can by trusting Jesus stand firm against the attacks of Satan, my great enemy (5:8-9).

After I have suffered a little while, my God, who is full of kindness through Christ, will give me His eternal glory. He personally will come and pick me up, and set me firmly in place, and make me stronger than ever (5:10).

To Him (God) be all power over all things, forever and ever. Amen (5:ll).

About the Author

Dr. French O'Shields and his wife, Alma, reside in Gaffney and Surfside Beach, South Carolina. They have four children, eight grandchildren and three great grandchildren. He is an ordained minister in the Presbyterian Church, U.S.A., Charlotte, North Carolina, Presbytery.

Education and training:
...B.S. in Psychology, University of South Carolina
...Summer school, graduate study in psychology, University of South Carolina
...M.Div., Erskine Theological Seminary
...D.Min., Union Theological Seminary, Richmond, Virginia
...Completed course, "Introduction to Psychiatry," along with medical students at Medical College of Georgia
...Completed course, "Hospital Pastoral Care," Presbyterian Hospital, Charlotte, North Carolina

Experience:
...Twenty-eight years as senior pastor of three Presbyterian Churches
...Taught Systematic Theology at Erskine Theological Seminary
...Over 100 hours attending and participating in weekly Psychiatric Staff Conference, Talmadge Memorial Hospital, Augusta, Georgia (Medical College of Georgia)
...Syndicated a weekly column in 20 newspapers in 4 states.

In 1982 he stopped pastoring churches due to a voice impairment (laryngeal dysphonia). His current ministry, presented through HEM OF HIS GARMENT, consists of writing, preaching/teaching engagements, and teaching his seminar on UNDERSTANDING, PREVENTING, AND OVERCOMING DEPRESSION in the United States and England.

Hem of His Garment

"And [they] besought him [Jesus] that they might touch the hem of his garment: and as many as touched were made perfectly whole" (Matthew 14:36, KJV).

HEM OF HIS GARMENT is a Christian ministry dedicated to the Glory of God and committed to encouraging and assisting individuals to discover and experience Christ's grace as sufficient for their desire and need to be made whole.

"My grace is all you need, for my power is greatest when you are weak." (The Lord's answer to Paul's prayer, 2 Corinthians 12:9, TEV.)

This ministry is presented through the teaching and writing of Dr. French O'Shields. His seminar UNDERSTANDING, PRE-VENTING, AND OVERCOMING DEPRESSION, speaking engagements, and additional copies of *Slaying the Giant* may be arranged and secured by writing to:

HEM OF HIS GARMENT
P.O. Box 14883
Surfside Beach, South Carolina 29587-4883

131

Comments From Others

"I'm forty-one years old and have lived with severe depression most of my adult life. I have been in the hospital four times for eight months and attempted suicide twice. I have read many books and listened to tapes and never found any answer to my problem. Your seminar has turned my life around. I am back at work and enjoy a totally different outlook on life."

A Business Man in Michigan

"Your material is well organized and presented in a helpful fashion. Your personal experience greatly enhances your ability to teach on depression and to inspire hope in others."

Dr. Randal L. Bremer
Presbyterian Pastor

"For the Lake City Ministerial Association and myself, I want to express our sincere appreciation to you for the seminar on depression. All the pastors participating were greatly helped in knowing how to help depressed persons."

The Reverend Don VanDyke, Pastor
Lake City, Michigan

"I have been intimately acquainted with depression in others. I am eternally grateful to you for collecting up all the scraps and presenting me with a cohesive body of knowledge with form and reason resolving all the conflicting ideas into a coherent meaningful whole."

Susan Sargcart
Norwich, England

"Your book is personally and professionally valuable to me. It is clear, meaningful, and the most beneficial of any I have read. It is a joy to share these practical solutions with others."

Sam Summey
Registered Nurse

"Thank you for sharing your seminar for our hospital's Community Health Program. Your overall presentation was excellent with participant verbal and written evaluation validating that assessment. We all benefited."

Debi S. McKenzie, R.N.
Georgetown (S.C.) Memorial Hospital

"Dr. O'Shields, be assured that all the suffering you endured during your depression God was molding you to be a messenger and a comforter for people like me. He kept you in that dark pit, until His divine purpose was accomplished just as the potter can put pieces of broken clay together. You had to pass the test He set before you. Your book ministered to the deepest parts of my mind and soul and put my life back together again."

T. M., Bank Officer
Charlotte, N.C.

"At a time when depression is a major health problem in this country, we desperately need a book to set forth a Christian perspective on depression. SLAYING THE GIANT by Dr. French O'Shields is that book. It is highly acclaimed and recommended by pastors, physicians, counselors, and depressives and their families who have been helped by it."

THE WINE PRESS, newsletter of CBU
Black Mountain, N.C.

"I recommend your book for anyone with depression. I especially like it because you speak with firsthand experience and provide a Scriptural answer."

A.D., Psychiatrist
Al.

"Personally and professionally, I find this book to be totally sound and highly useable without extraneous clinical jargon."

A.L., Psychiatric Nurse
S.C.

"I have concluded this is the best presentation on this subject I have read."
R.G., Clinical Psychologist
S.C.

"A profound piece of Biblical and experiential editing, a liberating book every pastor, counselor, and layman ought to have."
G.C., PhD, Marriage and Family Therapist
Fla.

"What a blessing your book has been to me. It has enabled me to give hope to depressed persons including some other missionaries."
S. P., Missionary
Kenya

"I am convinced God led me to your book in answer to prayer. Your book with the spiritual therapy has given me a new outlook on life."
S.T., Pa.

"People respond to this book more than any other."
B.B., Bookstore Owner
N.C.

"As a bookstore owner I know about many books on depression. This is the best I have read."
L. M., Bookstore Owner
S.C.

"May have more helpful information than any book I have seen on depression."
J.C., Editor, a Major Publisher
Va.

"I read a copy of Dr. O'Shields book that was loaned to me by my uncle. I must confess, I feel it was certainly sent to me through an angel because I would have never bought a book on depression. This book helped me understand my son so much better and also made me open my eyes up to myself. I am ordering a copy of the book for myself."

D. M.
Md.

"We are studying your book in our prayer/Bible Study group at my church. I want you to know how helpful it has been to each of us. Thanks for writing it."

L.L., an
Alabama Congregation

"You obviously know your subject and prove it over and over again. You are one of the best teachers I have heard on a difficult subject. Your presentation is clinically sound. You leave your readers full of hope."

Roque Fajardo, National Certified
Addiction Counselor-II

"What makes your seminar so special is you have gone through depression and returned to helping others by your insights on overcoming depresssion. I highly recommend it."

Elaine Townsend (Mrs. W. Cameron)
Wycliffe Bible Translators